THE TRUTH OF THE BIBLE

THE TRUTH
OF THE BIBLE

by
Oswald Loretz

HERDER AND HERDER

1968

HERDER AND HERDER NEW YORK

232 Madison Avenue, New York, N.Y. 10016

BURNS & OATES LIMITED

25 Ashley Place, London S.W. 1

Revised version of the original German edition:

"Die Wahrheit der Bibel", Herder, Freiburg 1964

Translated by David J. Bourke

Nihil obstat: Lionel Swain, S. T. L., L. S. S., Censor

Imprimatur: † Patrick Casey, Vic. Gen., Auxiliary Bishop of Westminster

Westminster, 27th February 1968.

Library of Congress Catalog Card Number: 68–13560

First published in West Germany © 1968, Herder KG

Printed in West Germany by Herder

CONTENTS

FOREWORD

The observations which follow are concerned with the question of the truth of Scripture. Their purpose is not to offer to the reader any definitive solutions, such as would leave no further light to be thrown on the problem of the truth of the Bible. They have a more limited aim than this. It is the author's intention to confine himself to the following aspect of the question: he wishes, insofar as the limits here indicated permit, to point out the deep significance of this question of the truth of the Bible and its relevance for us of the present day. For anyone who supposes that he can solve the special problems involved in the definitions of the truth of Scripture and the doctrine of inerrancy in the Church without regard to what the Bible has to say about the truth of God will sooner or later find himself in contradiction to Scripture itself. Anyone, on the other hand, who deepens his understanding of the statements in the Bible concerning God's truth will soon come to recognize that ultimately it is the Spirit of God who guides us into all truth (Jn 16:13), and that even within the Church this can never become mere 'subject-matter' which the human intellect can assimilate and make its own comprehensively and satisfyingly by its own efforts. On the contrary it is in the very nature of truth that it constantly represents for us not only light, but at one and the same time a question, a summons and a tormenting problem too, so that every age, ours not excluded, finds itself confronted anew with the question of truth in general and the question of the truth of Scripture in particular.

As was to be expected, the German version of this book has not met with universal agreement. The weight of theological tradition is still too strong for that. Yet against all the critics who might be mentioned here (L. Alonso-Schökel, *Bib* 46 [1965], pp. 378–80; E. Gutwenger, *ZKT* 87 [1965], pp. 196–8. The title of the article is significant: "Die Inerranz der Bibel"; K. H. Schelkle, *TQ* 145 [1965], pp. 362 f.; B. Brinkmann, *ThPh* 1 [1966], pp. 115–18) it must be maintained that what I am speaking of is (as is shown by the very title of this book) the *truth* of the Bible, and not its *inerrancy* or *freedom from error*. My intention was not to prove theology's doctrine of inerrancy, but to refute it.

Although the original edition of this book was published before the promulgation of the conciliar constitution *Dei Verbum,* concerning Scripture, nothing of what has been said here needs, in my view, to be deleted. The references to *Dei Verbum* which have been inserted in this new edition will show this to be the case. It will also be the best way of making clear what real progress *Dei Verbum* has contributed. Today it becomes one of the most important tasks of those engaged in interpreting Scripture to guard against any false interpretation of this deeply significant document.

For the English translation of my book my special thanks are due to Dr. D. J. Bourke of Burford, Oxfordshire.

Oswald Loretz

ABBREVIATIONS

AHW	*Akkadisches Handwörterbuch,* based on papers of Bruno Meissner (1868–1947), edited by W. von Soden (1959 ff.)
BF	K. Baltzer, *Das Bundesformular,* Wissenschaftliche Monographien zum Alten und Neuen Testament, vol. IV (1960)
Bib	*Biblica*
BiOr	*Bibliotheca Orientalis*
BZ	*Biblische Zeitschrift*
BZAW	*Beihefte zur Zeitschrift für die alttestamentliche Wissenschaft*
CBQ	*The Catholic Biblical Quarterly*
CSEL	*Corpus Scriptorum Ecclesiasticorum Latinorum*
DBS	*Dictionnaire de la Bible,* Supplément
DS	H. Denzinger and A. Schönmetzer, *Enchiridion Symbolorum* (32nd ed., 1963)
EB	*Enchiridion Biblicum* (3rd ed., 1958)
ETL	*Ephemerides Theologicae Lovanienses*
EvTh	*Evangelische Theologie*
GB	W. Genesius and F. Buhl, *Hebräisches und aramäisches Handwörterbuch über das Alte Testament* (17th ed., 1921)
HthG	*Handbuch theologischer Grundbegriffe,* edited by H. Fries and others, 2 vols. (1962–63)
HTR	*The Harvard Theological Review*
HZ	*Historische Zeitschrift*
JBL	*Journal of Biblical Literature*
JCS	*Journal of Cuneiform Studies*
JEOL	*Jahrbericht ex Oriente Lux*
JNES	*Journal of Near Eastern Studies*
KD	*Kerygma und Dogma*
KDB	*Kerygma und Dogma,* Beiheft [supplement] (*KDB* 1 = Offenbarung

	als Geschichte; edited by W. Pannenberg in collaboration with R. Rendtorff, U. Wilckens and T. Rendtorff; 2nd ed., 1963)
LTK	*Lexikon für Theologie und Kirche,* edited by J. Höfer and K. Rahner (2nd ed., 1957–65)
NRT	*Nouvelle Revue Théologique*
NT	*Novum Testamentum*
NTS	*New Testament Studies*
PEQ	*Palestine Exploration Quarterly*
PL	*Patrologia Latina,* edited by J. P. Migne (1878 ff.)
RB	*Revue Biblique*
RGG	*Die Religion in Geschichte und Gegenwart,* edited by K. Galling and others (3rd ed., 1957–62)
RScR	*Recherches de Science Religieuse*
ThBl	*Theologische Blätter*
ThPh	*Theologie und Philosophie*
ThRu	*Theologische Rundschau*
ThSt	*Theological Studies*
TLZ	*Theologische Literaturzeitung*
TQ	*Theologische Quartalschrift*
TrTZ	*Trierer theologische Zeitschrift*
TWNT	*Theologisches Wörterbuch zum Neuen Testament,* edited by G. Kittel and others (1933 ff.)
TZ	*Theologische Zeitschrift*
VD	*Verbum Domini*
VT	*Vetus Testamentum*
VTS	*Vetus Testamentum* — Supplements
ZAW	*Zeitschrift für die alttestamentliche Wissenschaft*
ZKT	*Zeitschrift für katholische Theologie*
ZNW	*Zeitschrift für die neutestamentliche Wissenschaft*
ZTK	*Zeitschrift für Theologie und Kirche*

INTRODUCTION

"For we cannot do anything against the truth, but only for the truth."   2 Cor 13:8.[1]

In current thought the problem of truth has once more come urgently to the fore. The forms in which it presents itself are manifold. It has not yet been disposed of either in the natural sciences or in art, in politics or in social life.[2] In the midst of the atomic age it appears in forms which are new and hitherto unknown, and it has an immediate importance for those who strive to direct their lives by religion.[3] Is it, then, really possible for theology to remain cut off from the world and unaffected by this problem?

A further point must be made in connection with the mediaeval solution of the problem of truth as expressed in the formula

---

[1] On the subject of 'the power of truth' cf. H. Blumenberg, "Die Metaphorik der 'mächtigen' Wahrheit", *Archiv für Begriffsgeschichte* 6 (1960), pp. 12–18.

[2] Growing attention is being paid to the problem of truth, which has been brought to the fore by the development of the natural sciences; cf. "La Vérité", *Actes du XIIe Congrès des Sociétés de Philosophie de Langue Française* (1964–65); K. Ulmer, ed., *Die Wissenschaften und die Wahrheit* (1966). Of decisive importance here is the position adopted by Galileo on the problem of truth. Cf. E. Kassirer, "Wahrheitsbegriff und Wahrheitsproblem bei Galilei", *Scientia* 62 (1937), pp. 121–30, 185–93; A. C. Crombie, "Galileo's Conception of Scientific Truth", *Literature and Science. Proceedings of the Sixth Triennial Congress, Oxford 1954* (1955), pp. 132–8; E. Namer, "La vérité dans les sciences depuis Galilée", *Actes du XIIe Congrès des Sociétés de Philosophie de Langue Française* (1964–65), pp. 129–33.

[3] R. Bultmann, "Der Gottesgedanke und der moderne Mensch", *ZTK* 60

adaequatio intellectus et rei.[4] If this formula were indeed sufficient the matter might rest there. In that case it would only be a question of smoothing out the inconsistencies that still remained. But however much exegetes may struggle to keep up appearances by pretending this to be the case, they still find themselves confronted inexorably with the problem of truth still unsolved. The form in which it presents itself to them is 'In what sense is the Bible true?' Certainly when the problem is presented in this way it does seem that the explanation put forward by the mediaeval schoolmen, so far from showing us how to solve it, actually places obstacles in our path. Our intention is, however, not to denigrate the scholastic movement but rather to notice certain consequences which are the end-products of a development initiated in part by scholasticism.[5] This is so in the sense that our modern concept of science can be traced back to a discussion which began among the scholastics themselves. This question has an important bearing on the problem of truth. As early as the thirteenth century the scholars who were discussing it arrived at conclusions the full significance of which only emerged with the introduction of empirical methods by Galileo.[6]

(1963), p. 343, penetratingly remarks upon the fact that for the life of faith of modern man the question of truth is of decisive importance, and that it cannot be viewed in abstraction from the relation of modern man to the world. In this connection Bultmann adduces a statement of Vahanian, who says in *The Death of God. The Culture of Our Post-Christian Era* (1961), p. 11, that the problem for Christianity is how to find the correlation between the truth of Christianity and the empirical truths by which men live without confusing them; man cannot live by one of these truths alone without the other.

[4] On the history of this definition see H. Blumenberg, "Paradigmen zu einer Metaphorologie", *Archiv für Begriffsgeschichte* 6 (1960), p. 12, n. 2a. The formula is derived from Avicenna. cf. H. Pouillon, "Le premier Traité des Propriétés transcendentales. La 'Summa de bono' in Chancelier Philippe", *Revue Néoscolastique de Philosophie* 42 (1939), pp. 57ff.

[5] P. Wilpert, "Wissenschaft und Wahrheit im Mittelalter" in *L'homme et son destin d'après les penseurs du moyen âge* (1960), pp. 51–69.

[6] On the mathematical forms of expression employed in systems of modern physics and on the manner in which theory and experiment are combined see

Regarded historically we find ourselves confronted with the task of answering the questions relating to the truth of the Bible which Galileo raised in a manner which could not be ignored, and which have become still more pressing with the progress achieved in the natural sciences.[7] The Church finds herself faced not only with the question of how the gospel is to be preached to the people of Asia and Africa but also with the no less pressing question, how is her message to be addressed to that section of civilized society which has been moulded by natural science? Since the trial of Galileo the truth of the Bible has been a matter for debate to an extent unknown before his time.

So far as exegesis is concerned the effect of this altered state of the question is that it now becomes necessary to think out the problem of the truth of the Bible on an entirely new basis. If dogmatic theology shows itself none too ready to collaborate with exegesis in this task, that fact only serves to make it all the clearer how absolutely necessary it is today to return to the sources of theology, that is to sacred scripture itself.[8]

Today it is possible once more to recognize that the problem of the truth of Scripture has long been thrust into the background by theologians, to make way for the problem of inspiration. It cannot be denied that this procedure is connected with the taking

J. Kolb, "Erfahrung im Experiment und in der Theorie der Physik" in W. Strolz, ed., *Experiment und Erfahrung in Wissenschaft und Kunst* (1963), pp. 9ff. On the significance of hypotheses see G. Holton, "Über die Hypothesen, welche der Naturwissenschaft zugrunde liegen", *Eranos* 31 (1962–63), pp. 351ff., W. Braunbek, "Wie gewinnt die Physik ihre Erkenntnis?", *Wissenschaft und Weisheit*, pp. 34–47.

[7] For the problem of biblical truth as well as in other respects the central importance of Galileo Galilei is becoming more and more recognized. Cf. A. M. Dubarle, "Les principes exégétiques et théologiques de Galilée concernant la science de la nature", *Revue des Sciences Philosophiques et Théologiques* 50 (1966), pp. 67–87; O. Loretz, *Galilei und der Irrtum der Inquisition* (1966).

[8] On the current discussion concerning the relationship between dogma and exegesis see J. Blenkinsopp, "Biblical and Dogmatic Theology, the Present Situation", *CBQ* 26 (1964), pp. 70–85.

over of rabbinical and Mohammedan theories concerning the nature of prophetism.[9] The taking over of these extra-biblical views and also the attitude of mediaeval schoolmen to the problem of truth (an attitude based on the logic of being which held the field at the period in question) led to certain assertions concerning the truth of Scripture. These assertions can be re-affirmed today

[9] On the question of inspiration in general cf. G. Lanczkowski, O. Weber, W. Philipp, "Inspiration", *RGG* (1959), cols. 773–82; A. Bea, "Inspiration", *LTK,* vol. V, cols. 703–11; P. Grelot, "L'Inspiration scripturaire", *RScR* 51 (1963), pp. 337–82; P. Benoît, "Révélation et Inspiration", *RB* 70 (1963), pp. 321–70. Although knowledge has been acquired of the particular philosophical presuppositions on which the doctrine of inspiration depends, and of the influence of Jewish and Arabian circles on scholastic positions with regard to it, this knowledge has not really been brought to fruition in recent presentations of the subject, and particularly in the treatment of prophetism. Cf. J. Guttmann, *Moses ben Maimon I* (1908), pp. 197 ff. On scholastic teaching on prophetism and its historical background cf. B. Decker, *Die Entwicklung der Lehre der prophetischen Offenbarung von Wilhelm von Auxerre bis zu Thomas von Aquin* (1940); J. M. Casciare, "Contribución al estudio de las fuentes árabes y rabínicas en la doctrina de Santo Tomás sobre la profecía", *Estudios Bíblicos* 18 (1959), pp. 117–48; E. I. J. Rosenthal, *Griechisches Erbe in der jüdischen Religionsphilosophie des Mittelalters* (1960), pp. 55–68, 79–86; M. E. Marmura, "Avicenna's Psychological Proof of Prophecy", *JNES* 22 (1963), pp. 49–56. In 1 Pet 1:10–12 we find teaching on the origin of the prophetic writings and on how they are filled with the Holy Spirit. On the connection between this teaching and the views found in late Judaism see K. H. Schelkle, "Hermeneutische Zeugnisse im Neuen Testament", *BZ* 6 (1962), pp. 172–75. The theories of inspiration currently taught in seminaries etc. either provide no answer at all, or at most highly unsatisfactory answers, on important problems of exegesis. On the problem of whether it is only the final author or the earlier 'authors' too who were inspired cf. J. A. McKenzie, "The Social Character of Inspiration", *CBQ* 24 (1962), pp. 115–24. This author rightly points out that one cannot simply assume without argument that it was only the final author or redactor of a document of the Bible who was inspired. There are cases in which this theory, so much favoured in current study, is irreconcilable with the data actually contained in the Bible, cf. e.g. B. E. Haenchen, "Probleme des johanneischen 'Prologs'", *ZTK* 60 (1963), p. 332, n. 95. Against McKenzie D. J. MacCarthy emphasizes the part played by the personality of the individual author in the production of a literary work.

only by those who in unthinking security fail to recognize the historical development involved.[10]

In this connection the part played by Augustine becomes important. cf. H. Sasse, "Sacra Scriptura — Bemerkungen zur Inspirationslehre Augustins" in *Festschrift Franz Dornseiff* (1953), pp. 262–73. Sasse's judgment on Augustine's doctrine of inspiration is based on solid grounds: "Under the authority of the greatest of the Fathers of the Church Christendom adopted a theory of the inspiration of sacred writings which is only a pagan doctrine forced with difficulty into a 'christianized' form. That it has had to drag this along with it through the centuries is one of the great tragedies of the history of the Church" (p. 267). According to Augustine, who on this point is under the influence of pagan theories of inspiration, inspiration is to be understood as meaning "that man is only the instrument of the Holy Spirit and that the latter alone determined the content and the form of Scripture. From this it follows as a general rule that the Bible is free from mistakes, errors and contradictions even in its smallest details" (Sasse, *ibid.,* p. 269). Because of holding this theory Augustine had to explain away the difficulties which the real facts presented him with. He could do this only by having recourse to the idea of a 'deeper sense' which he presumed to be present. All this followed from his unbiblical concepts of truth and inspiration (for specific examples cf. Sasse, *ibid.,* pp. 269 ff.). Sasse comes to the following conclusion: "We must content ourselves with these examples and attempt to answer the question,

---

[10] Right at the outset of this work attention must be drawn to the following factor in our approach: in the course of this exposition there can be no question of approaching the problem of biblical truth dialectically, and so of emphasizing any one particular aspect of truth at the expense of others, or, for instance, of saying that the Greek concept of truth, as against the Hebrew, is to be rejected. Our purpose is rather to point out that both theology and exegesis operate to their own disadvantage when they pay too little attention to what the Bible calls 'truth' in its full range of significance, and when they substitute some other concept of truth for that contained in the Bible.

'What lesson it to be drawn from Augustine's attempt to prove the inerrancy of sacred Scripture apologetically?' It shows that it is impossible to apply to the Bible that concept of inspiration which is based on Hellenistic, pagan and Jewish ideas, and according to which the Spirit of God uses man as his completely passive instrument. For in fact even the great Father of the Church was never able to adduce any proof for the immunity from error which he ascribed to the Scriptures. He sought to maintain his position either by clumsy attempts at harmonization, as in the case of the cleansing of the temple or the hour of the crucifixion, attempts which convince no-one and which are historically impossible; or else he found himself compelled to take refuge in a *res velata mysteriis* present in Scripture, and in a *secretius consilium providentiae Dei* which would have guided the biblical authors" (*ibid.,* p. 272). The influence of Augustine on the Christian doctrine of inspiration may be compared with the not altogether fortunate effects which his teaching has had on the Christian ethics of marriage (on this see H. Klemps, *Ehemoral und Jansenismus* [1964], pp. 11 ff.).[11]

The time is now ripe for us to see that the idea of the truth of Scripture has further and deeper implications than its immunity from error (inerrantia) as understood by scholastic theology.

---

[11] L. Alonso-Schökel (*Bib* 46 [1945], pp. 378 f.) is of the opinion that Augustine allows for the presence in sacred Scripture of statements which we would today describe as *errores*. In this L. Alonso-Schökel is probably shifting the point of the argument unjustifiably. For when Augustine suggests that particular difficulties are to be solved by having recourse to the rule *Spiritus Sanctus ... alium sic, alium vero sic narrationem suam ordinare persuaserit* (*PL,* XXXIV, col. 1102), his intention is to deny the presence of what we call an error, and this has nothing to do with the totally different question of whether the biblical author was or was not a lifeless instrument in the hand of God. According to the soundly based view of the experts Augustine maintains the inerrancy of sacred Scripture as a firm and irrefutable principle. (Cf. J. Schildenberger, *Augustinus Magister,* vol. II [1954], p. 677; K. Lorenz, "Die Wissenschaftslehre des Augustinus", *Zeitschrift für Kirchengeschichte* 67 [1955/56], p. 221, n. 75.)

Again this inerrancy is to be understood as a mere necessary logical deduction, a consequence — albeit the principal one — of inspiration.[12]

The question of inspiration can become meaningful once more only when we have understood what Scripture has to say concerning *the truth of God*. The question today is no longer "How shall I, on the basis of the doctrine of inspiration, cope with the arduous problem of the truth of Scripture?", but instead this: *"How does a doctrine of inspiration appear which takes cognizance of the statements in Scripture concerning truth?"*

If, therefore, in the pages which follow, the question of inspiration appears to be neglected, this has been done deliberately. It is presupposed that Scripture is divinely inspired, but what is called in question is whether any of the theories so far formulated in theology can be reconciled satisfactorily with the evidence of Scripture itself.

In *Dei Verbum* the deduction is drawn from the doctrine of inspiration that sacred Scripture is true in a special sense (cf. III, art. 11, "Cum ergo . . ." to ". . . instructus"). Thus the effect of the inspiration of the books is no longer seen as *inerrancy* (as it has been hitherto in the books of theological instruction

---

[12] Cf., for example, A. Bea in *Institutiones Biblicae*, vol. I (1951), p. 85: "Effectus principalis inspirationis est *inerrantia* ss. liborum." E. Gutwenger in *ZKT* 87 (1965), p. 196, deduces the inerrancy of Scripture from inspiration "by the use of syllogisms". Bruce Vawter, "The Fuller Sense: Some Considerations", *CBQ* 26 (1964), p. 93, n. 15, points out ". . . that instrumental causality as the sole or adequate theological explanation of inspiration is not part of the Church's teaching". Vawter then continues: "The Church has endorsed the analogy for its virtues (cf. *EB* 556), not for what it cannot do, or for what it does ineptly. It is at least conceivable that the further development of theology could make it both possible and imperative to abandon this analogy entirely." That the 'theory of instrumentality' was not defined at Vatican I is shown by N. Weyns, "De notione inspirationis biblicae juxta Concilium Vaticanum", *Angelicum* 30 (1953), pp. 315–66. For the cautious formulation of Vatican II see *Dei Verbum,* ch. III, art. 11.

and the encyclicals[13] but *truth*. Viewed in the perspective of theological discussion up till now these words of the Council are of fundamental importance; here for the first time an attempt is made to give a positive answer to the really outstanding problem of the truth of the Bible.

In this connection it is significant from an historical point of view that Vatican II is the first Council to treat *expressis verbis* of the question of the immunity of the Bible from error, and to arrive at the solution that the Bible imparts truth to us and not that it is first and foremost to be regarded as a document immune from error. On this point Vatican II attaches itself to the conciliar tradition of the Church in the following manner: 1) The Council of Florence: God is the author of the Old and New Testaments; 2) Trent: the relation of Scripture to Tradition; 3) Vatican I: Inspiration, and Vatican II: The truth of sacred Scripture.[14]

[13] The meaning of the constitution *Dei Verbum* is in danger of being distorted by those who overlook the element in this document that is new. Thus, for instance, it is said that Chapter III, which has a decisive bearing upon the questions of the inspiration and interpretation of Scripture, has hardly anything to contribute which goes beyond the traditional theological views (e.g. H. Vorgrimler in *Bibel und Liturgie* 39 [1966], p. 109).

[14] For references to the sources cf. Loretz, *Galilei,* pp. 182 f.

CHAPTER ONE

PROBLEM OF THE TRUTH OF SCRIPTURE AND REVELATION

The Church holds fast to the writings comprising the Old and New Testaments as the book containing revelation from God, and she takes this word of God as the basis for her message and her life. For this reason the Bible is accorded a unique place in the Church, and one which can be taken by nothing else.[1]

The reader who really ponders the statements contained in the books of the Old and New Testaments is led by them into an inescapable position: the Bible, which is handed over to us as the word of God, is nevertheless a book in which men speak. Granted, what is spoken of by the men who address us in this book is the fact that God has spoken to them in such and such

---

[1] K. H. Schelkle, "Die Bibel in der Kirche" in L. Klein, ed., *Diskussion über die Bibel* (1963), pp. 99–113. The question of whether the whole of revelation is contained in Scripture is not of immediate concern in the present context. For what is primarily in question here is simply the relationship between Scripture and revelation. On the controversy concerning the sufficiency of Scripture cf. J. P. Mackey, *The Modern Theology of Tradition* (1962), pp. 150–65; G. Moran, *Scripture and Tradition, a Survey of the Controversy* (1963); P. Rusch, "De non definienda illimitata insufficientia materiali Scripturae", *ZKT* 85 (1963), pp. 1–15; H. Schauf, *Die Lehre der Kirche über Schrift und Tradition in den Katechismen* (1963), pp. 7 ff.; J. Beumer, "Schriftbeweis und Traditionsbeweis", *Theologie und Glaube* 54 (1964), pp. 1–9; and the bibliography of recent work provided by these authors. No decision on this question is to be found in *Dei Verbum,* ch. III, art. 11, cf. *Schema Constitutionis de Divina Revelatione* (1964), p. 30: '. . . *ne dirimatur quaestio disputata de habitudine inter S. Scripturam et Traditionem.*'

a manner; but even in those instances in which Scripture itself expressly states that God speaks directly to man, the fact still remains that *our* information on this event comes to us only in the form of *human* words. Hence K. H. Schelkle is perfectly right in prefixing the following observation to his essay, "Sacred Scripture and Word of God": "We call Sacred Scripture God's word. But when we try to catch this word in the Scripture what do we hear? Not the direct *word* in the helpful evidence of divine and life-laden truth; directly, only the *Scripture* is given us, one book among many, and indeed a book, as regards the New Testament at any rate, that has no claim at all to be placed among the great works of literature."[2] Inevitably, therefore, we find ourselves, by the very fact of explaining that Scripture is the word of God, faced with the difficult task of pointing out where in this book, that contains nothing but human words, God still utters his own true word, interposes his deeds, and in this manner imparts something that goes beyond human knowledge, human decisions and human designs, something, therefore, that constitutes a revelation of himself.[3]

For the primary reason why Scripture carries relevance and authority for us can only be that more is expressed in it than ideas about the world and the relationship of God to man, thought out by individuals or whole generations thousands of years before. If this were all that was to be found in Scripture then the

---

[2] K. H. Schelkle in H. Vorgrimler, ed., *Dogmatic versus Biblical Theology* (1964), p. 11. Further on this cf. G. Bornkamm, "Gotteswort und Menschenwort im Neuen Testament" in *Studien zu Antike und Urchristentum* (1959), pp. 223–36.
[3] Here we are presupposing that concept of revelation which underlies the passage of Heb 1:1 ff. In the course of our treatment we shall have to establish more closely what the general background of this concept is, and how it should be regarded in the light of this. On the concept of revelation in current theology the following works are enlightening: W. Bulst, *Offenbarung. Biblischer und theologischer Begriff* (1960), pp. 11 ff.; J. R. Geiselmann, "Offenbarung", *HthG,* vol. II (1963), pp. 242–50; G. Gloege, *RGG,* IV (1960), cols. 1609–13; R. Schnackenburg – H. Fries, "Offenbarung", *LTK,* vol. VII, cols. 1106–15; R. Latourelle, *Théologie de la Révélation* (1963).

most it could still lay claim to would be some sort of place of honour in the history of religions. But from the viewpoint of contemporary man it would have to be regarded as belonging finally and irrevocably to the past.[4] The force of the biblical message can be made effective in the present only if what it contains is the very *truth* of God; not, however, the truth of God in a sense in which it can be reduced to an ideological concept of philosophy or theology, but the truth that decides between light and darkness, death and life. Thus the question confronting us is: "In what sense is the Bible the book in which God addresses truth to us?" Apart from the fact that the only words we find in Scripture are human ones, a further circumstance which prevents us from coming too quickly to an understanding of the question of biblical and revealed truth is the fact that Scripture itself knows of no revelational terminology which is well-established and unambiguous. There is not a single passage in Scripture, therefore, which provides us with a concept of revelation which is unequivocal or completely comprehensible to us.

In the Old Testament, then, we find several words used to describe the divine act of self-revelation; they emphasize now one and now another aspect of this self-revelation.[5] Thus for instance we find mention of God's act of 'unveiling, uncovering' *(gālah)*,[6] allowing himself to be 'known' *(yāda')*,[7] 'manifesting

---

[4] Among others J. Huxley, *Religion without Revelation* (2nd ed., 1961), p. 88 adopts this position: "There are three recognized ways of approach towards the intellectual comprehension and definition of the term God. One may simply point to the so-called revelation of Scripture. Since this to me and to most educated men and women today is simply an appeal to mythology, I did not concern myself with it."

[5] Cf. H. Haag, " 'Offenbaren' in der hebräischen Bibel", *TZ* 16 (1960), pp. 251–8; R. Rendtorff, "Die Offenbarungsvorstellungen im Alten Israel", *KDB* 1, pp. 21–41; W. Zimmerli, " 'Offenbarung' im Alten Testament", *EvTh* 22 (1962), pp. 15–31.

[6] Haag, "Offenbaren", pp. 251 ff., Rendtorff, "Offenbarungsvorstellungen", p. 23; Zimmerli, "Offenbarung im AT", p. 16.

[7] Haag, "Offenbaren", pp. 254 ff.

himself' *(hingîd)*,[8] and 'showing himself, appearing' *(nir'āh)*,[9] the 'manifestation of his glory',[10] and the 'declaring of himself' or 'disclosure of himself' on Yahweh's part, indicated by the formula *'anokî Yahweh', *'I am Yahweh (your God)'.[11]

This manner of speaking in several different ways of the revelatory activity of God is traditional in the Old Testament and is also continued in the New, so that here too "no unified and firmly established terminology for the divine 'revelation' is employed".[12] The New Testament follows the Old in describing the revelatory activity of God as a 'speaking',[13] an 'unveiling',[14] 'making known'

[8] *Ibid.,* pp. 256 ff.

[9] Rendtorff, "Offenbarungsvorstellungen", pp. 23 ff.; F. Schnutenhaus, *ZAW* 76 (1964), pp. 10 ff.

[10] Rendtorff, "Offenbarungsvorstellungen", pp. 28 ff.

[11] *Ibid.,* pp. 32 ff.; Zimmerli, "Offenbarung im AT", pp. 18 ff.; J. Lindblom, "Die Vorstellung vom Sprechen Jahwes zu den Menschen im Alten Testament", *ZAW* 75 (1963), pp. 263–88. This author examines the various ways in which, as the Old Testament sees it, God came near to men in order to speak to them. Lindblom sums up the results of his investigation as follows: "He (God) could speak to them 'face to face' as one man speaks to another. He spoke through the medium of dreams, visions in the sanctuary, omens and sacred lots, by means of events in the natural order and in human life, through seers and prophets who had themselves received the message addressed to them by God only when they had been interiorly inspired by the laws, these being regarded as the word of God. Thus we can lay it down as a characteristic trait of Old Testament piety that whatever the circumstances might be, Hebrew man always found himself in a position to ascertain God's will, his thoughts and intentions, as these applied in various cases. In the theocentric religion of the Old Testament the idea of God's transcendence was always tempered by that of his proximity. An example of this is the fact that Yahweh spoke to men" *(ibid.,* p. 287). Certain aspects of the manner in which revelation was unfolded are discussed by H. Gross, "Zur Offenbarungsentwicklung im Alten Testament" in *Gott in Welt, Festgabe für Karl Rahner,* vol. I (1964), pp. 407–22.

[12] R. Schnackenburg, "Zum Offenbarungsgedanken in der Bibel", *BZ* 7 (1963), p. 2. See also H. Schulte, *Der Begriff der Offenbarung im Neuen Testament* (1949), pp. 34–84.

[13] R. Kittel, λέγω, *TWNT,* vol. IV, pp. 105 ff.

[14] A. Oepke, ἀποκαλύπτω, *TWNT,* vol. III, pp. 565–97.

(γνωρίζειν),[15] and 'disclosing, manifesting' (δηλοῦν,[16] φανεροῦν,[17] ἐμφανίζειν[18]) on the part of God. In the Johannine gospel, the formula by which Yahweh proclaims himself in the Old Testament is taken up and applied in a newer way in the phrase ἐγώ εἰμι.[19]

There is a further difficulty in addition to the one indicated above in finding an unambiguous term in Scripture for the revelation of God. It is the difficulty that it is no longer possible naively to identify Scripture with revelation because it is the word of God. For more recent exegesis has shown that Scripture also gives us a kind of knowledge which is demonstrably not revealed, but was developed and fostered within the Israelite community itself, or taken over from neighbouring peoples. In other words it has become impossible to regard Scripture and revelation as constituting a single entity in the sense that the former is directly identified in all that it says with the truth of God.

Progress in research into the world of the ancient Near East makes it impossible, e.g. mentally to assign to Scripture a place apart as though it were far above all other literatures, and in relation to them had an independent existence of its own. For instance J. Brinktrine, in considering the revelational character of the Old Testament and its credibility follows the line of traditional apologetics in regarding it as "the product of a mind that has a well cultivated sense of history".[20] According to

---

[15] R. Bultmann, *TWNT,* vol. I, p. 718.

[16] R. Bultmann, *TWNT,* vol. II, pp. 2, 60 ff.

[17] See provisionally W. Arndt and F. Gingrich, eds., *A Greek-English Lexicon of the New Testament* (1957), *sub voce.*

[18] *Ibid.*

[19] H. Zimmermann, "Das absolute Ἐγώ εἰμι als die neutestamentliche Offenbarungsformel", *BZ* 4 (1960), pp. 54–69, 266–76.

[20] J. Brinktrine, *Offenbarung und Kirche,* vol. II (2nd ed., 1949), p. 3. It would also be possible to adduce authors who speak still more openly in this vein when confronted with the problems of exegesis. But the observations of Brinktrine throw all the light that could be desired on the *status quaestionis.*

Brinktrine this is to be seen "in the exactitude with which the list of the genealogies is traced and verified . . .".[21] No less unfortunate is the view which Brinktrine expresses to the effect that 'the outlook of Genesis 1–11, being universalist, religious, moral, and monotheistic, tells against the supposition that it depends upon borrowing from extra-biblical cultures'.[22] And he

That it is necessary to present the problem with all possible clarity is shown precisely by more recent works such as P. Grelot's "Études sur la théologie du Livre Saint", *NRT* 85 (1963), pp. 785–806, 897–925, and P. Benoît, "Révélation et Inspiration", *RB* 70 (1963), pp. 321–70. Since Grelot (p. 924) concludes that the principle *Quidquid in sacra Scriptura continetur verum est* can still be upheld, he must have overlooked the fact that the theological formula to which he adheres is, historically speaking, extremely biassed (cf. p. 3, n. 8). Moreover, with reference to the problem of the truth of Scripture Grelot is inclined to attach too much importance to the question of literary *genres*. The literary form in which a matter is presented is the artificial medium in which truth is articulated, but it is an oversimplification and error to *identify* the truth that is being expressed or pointed to with the artificial form itself. Grelot does oversimplify the problem of truth to which the artificial mode (in this case literary) of expression gives rise. For a discussion of literary and non-literary modes of expression see, among others, M. Heidegger, *Nietzsche,* vol. I (1961), pp. 166 ff., 189 ff., 218 ff., 243 ff.; B. Allemann, "Experiment und Erfahrung in der Gegenwartsliteratur" in W. Strolz, ed., *Experiment und Erfahrung in Wissenschaft und Kunst* (1963), pp. 266 ff.; C. Pack, "Das Experiment in der bildenden Kunst — Kunst als Experiment", *ibid.,* pp. 185 ff. See further *infra* p. 84, n. 29. On the special question of the truth of poetry cf. J.-E. Heyde, "Διὸ ποίησις καὶ φιλοσοφώτερον καὶ σπουδαιότερον ἱστορίας ἐστίν, Aristoteles Poetik c. 9 (1451 b 6). Ein Beitrag zur Geschichte des Wortes φιλοσοφία", in G. Erdmann and A. Eichstaedt, eds., *Worte und Werte, B. Markwardt zum 60. Geburtstag* (1961), pp. 123–41; Heyde translates: "Poetry is both more akin to science and more meaningful than history" (*ibid.,* p. 136); W. Kayser, *Die Wahrheit der Dichter. Wandlung eines Begriffes in der deutschen Literatur* (1961); R. Bachem, *Dichtung als verborgene Theologie* (1956); O. Pöggeler, "Dichtungstheorie und Toposforschung", *Jahrbuch für Ästhetik und Allgemeine Kunstwissenschaft* V (1960), pp. 125 ff., W. Veit, "Toposforschung. Forschungsbericht", *Deutsche Vierteljahrschrift für Literaturwissenschaft und Geistesgeschichte* 37 (1963), pp. 184 ff.; E. Zinn, "Wahrheit in Philosophie und Dichtung", *Wissenschaft und Weisheit,* pp. 134–52.

[21] Brinktrine, *Offenbarung und Kirche,* p. 3.   [22] *Ibid.,* p. 5.

goes on to say: 'These traits are peculiar to the biblical narrative, and if we suppose that borrowing has taken place, they remain an insoluble mystery. Even from the purely scientific standpoint, therefore, it is most probable that the primeval history represents part of the ancient tradition of the human race'.[23] Brinktrine falls into further great difficulties when he attempts to defend the revelational character of the Old Testament by refusing to allow objections to its moral teaching. For instance in dependence upon Thomas Aquinas he conjures up a God who dispenses from the natural law.[24] In this way a smooth explanation can be found for such episodes as Abraham's projected slaying of his son. When the Israelites are condemned for inhuman cruelty towards the Canaanite cities conquered by them, J. Brinktrine imagines that he can dispose of this objection merely by observing 'that the extermination of the population of Canaan had been expressly prescribed by God', and that therefore the Israelites were 'neither unjust nor cruel when they sought to annihilate the Canaanite tribes. Israel did her duty; she was only carrying out what God had ordered her to do'.[25] In the light of contemporary research there is no need to spend much time in demonstrating the flaws in the arguments put forward by Brinktrine. He found it necessary to adduce these arguments in order to defend the truth of the Bible and its revelational character!

No one, therefore, can seriously attempt to cite the genealogies of the Bible as an example proving that the history contained in it is especially reliable.[26] Again with regard to the question of

---

[23] *Ibid.*
[24] *Ibid.,* p. 13; J. Messner, "Naturrechtswidrigkeiten im Alten Testament?" in *Jahrbuch des Instituts für christliche Sozialwissenschaft,* III (1962), pp. 109–22. This author examines the Thomist theory of dispensation from the natural law, and attempts a new solution to the problem of the features in the Old Testament which are contrary to it. He does this by placing a stronger emphasis on the idea of development.
[25] Brinktrine, *Offenbarung und Kirche,* p. 15.
[26] On the problem of the Babylonian, Canaanite and Hebrew genealogies cf.,

borrowings in Genesis 1–11 it must be said in passing that here Israel is dependent upon her neighbours. The portrait of the world found in the creation narratives, and the account of the first man can be understood only against the background of ancient Near Eastern lore which belongs to them. In the same way the narrative of the Flood — to take only one example — was demonstrably known to tradition long before Israel came into existence as a people.[27] In his fascination with the natural law J. Brinktrine overlooks, in his treatment of Genesis 21 (the sacrifice of Isaac), the possibility that the idea or the memory of human sacrifice may have played its part in this account.[28] Again, he fails to observe that the cruelty with which the Israelites waged their wars was in accordance with the laws and customs of the time, and that it cannot simply be seen as the result of the command of God.[29] Otherwise it would be possible to excuse the cruelties of the Assyrians in the same way, since their kings were likewise called to wage war at the divine behest.[30]

Moreover, because of the distinctions drawn in scholastically orientated theology it was formerly possible to produce solutions to difficulties which, while well adapted to the general theological system of the time, must today be considered *a priori* and artificial. By way of example let us take an answer given by Thomas Aquinas to the objection that certain of the truths imparted at Sinai (the existence of God, certain commandments) could be apprehended by the human reason even without a special revel-

e.g., J. J. Finkelstein, "The Antediluvian Kings: a University of California Tablet", *JCS* 17 (1963), p. 50, n. 41.

[27] Cf., e.g., E. Sollberger, *The Babylonian Legend of the Flood* (1962).

[28] Cf. L. Rost, "Erwägungen zum israelitischen Brandopfer", *BZAW* 77 (1958), pp. 181 f.; R. de Vaux, *Les sacrifices de l' Ancien Testament* (1964), p. 62. On the special question of the Israelite š lamîm sacrifices and their pre-Israelite and biblical history see R. Schmidt, *Das Bundesopfer in Israel. Wesen, Ursprung und Bedeutung der alttestamentlichen Schelamim* (1964).

[29] Cf. C. H. W. Brekelmans, *De Ḥerem in het Oude Testament* (1959), pp. 189 f.

[30] Cf. F. R. Kraus, "Assirisch Imperialisme", *JEOL* XV (1957–58), pp. 232–48.

16

ation from God (cf. *Contra Gent.* I, IV). Aquinas replies that God revealed these *praeambula fidei*[31] not in order to impart them as things wholly unknowable, but in order to render these truths, which the human reason can arrive at only with difficulty, easy for man to perceive and accept with confidence.

It must be admitted that this did resolve the difficulty as felt at that time. But the situation was transformed the moment it was realized that the prescriptions of the Mosaic law were representative of a jurisprudence which was general and widespread, and which was included in Scripture because it was already available at the time when the covenant was made, or else because it was subsequently added on to the laws. It was also realized that the truths themselves were subject to change and increase in the course of time in a manner which was customary everywhere.[32] Now for modern historically orientated exegesis the traditional refusal to admit the force of the above-mentioned objection is entirely unjustified. For the system of law with which Israel was already familiar at the time at which God revealed himself to her at Sinai cannot be considered as part of this revelation.

The examples which we have chosen will suffice to show that it has become impossible to defend the position in which Scripture is too hastily identified with divine revelation. This position is one in which Scripture is regarded as the document of revelation in the sense that it is explained as independent of any other human tradition and as spiritually and morally justified in every conceivable case. Similarly it is no longer possible to explain as revealed truth that which is manifestly of pre-Israelite or extra-Israelite origin. Statements, ideas and images which were formerly

---

[31] On the Thomist doctrine of the *praeambula fidei* cf. G. de Broglie, "La vraie notion thomiste de 'praeambula fidei'", *Gregorianum* 34 (1953), pp. 341–89; id., "Précisions complémentaires à propos de la notion thomiste de 'praeambula fidei'", *Gregorianum* 36 (1965), pp. 291 ff.; A. Lang, *Die Entfaltung des apologetischen Problems in der Scholastik des Mittelalters* (1962), pp. 58 f., 94 ff.

[32] On the biblical laws cf. pp. 65–66.

thought to belong to Scripture alone have now been shown to belong to a large extent to a heritage which Israel held in common with her neighbours, and which was known to others besides herself. It has been demonstrated more and more forcibly that the Bible is to be viewed in the light of its cultural environment. This book, then, limited as it is to a particular period, and belonging as it does to a broader historical context, can no longer be regarded without further qualification as revelation. And if this is the case, then the question is raised anew '*How?*' and '*Where?*' is divine revelation present in Scripture?

Thus we have arrived once more at the questions 'What is true in the Bible?', 'Where does God speak to us?'; we are not merely confronted with a collection of writings which record certain customs and certain events of the past. On the one hand, therefore, it is established beyond all denial that progress in scientific history has resulted in a certain secularization of Scripture.[33] But on the other hand it is no less unmistakably apparent that the problem of truth is not thereby *disposed of but only raised again in a new form.* In this respect biblical interpretation is faced with the same problem of truth as other scientific disciplines which, in the same way, have constantly to view the problem of truth in a fresh light.[34]

But at the same time this is precisely the point at which confusion of spirit supervenes. The more recent exegesis is felt to be an instigator of unrest; it overthrows established positions. Exegesis itself finds itself subject to constant fluctuations, and its attention is wholly taken up with correcting itself. To the onlooker from outside it seems as though a period of the wildest subjectivism has begun, which no longer leaves any truth undisturbed or unaffected.

It is true to say that exegesis gives the same impression to those who are more immediately occupied with the questions

[33] Baumgartner, "Die Auslegung des Alten Testaments im Streit der Gegenwart", in *Zum Alten Testament und seiner Umwelt* (1959), p. 180.
[34] Cf. the articles assembled in *Wissenschaft und Weisheit*.

formulated above. The only question is how this phenomenon should be regarded. In its restless fluctuations exegesis manifests a symptom which it has in common with modern intellectual life in general, and to which exegesis itself is subject by reason of its manifold involvements with the historical sciences.[35] For since "history at any given period is viewed as from the present", it shares in "the changeability of the present mode of existence".[36] For this reason it can "from the outset be apprehended objectively only by a process of constant re-appraisal".[37] This is not to be understood as subjectivism. For in a world that is historically conditioned, and has been recognized as subject, of its very nature, to the limitations of time, "the idea of an objective truth which is yet subject to re-appraisal can no longer surprise us".[38] The openness of history to fresh events and decisions which modify its course implies that what is past "is filled out by the accretion of new events, and the new fulness which history acquires by being broadened in this manner makes it susceptible of new emphases and new 'evaluations'. These, then, are not subjective preferences, but are objectively based upon history itself. Fresh significances are perceived, perhaps, in the light of freshly acquired or freshly observed data; or even fresh judgments are made, based on modifications of one's view of the past as an integral whole."[39]

The outcome of all this is that in the light of the developments of the modern science of history exegesis is right to have quitted its former peaceful existence; and since it thereby shares in a more general symptom of modern intellectual life it is idle to regard what is taking place in it as the effect of a wanton stirring

---

[35] For an exposition that goes to the root of the problem cf. A. Mirgeler, "Erfahrung in der Geschichte und Geschichtswissenschaft" in W. Strolz, ed., *Experiment und Erfahrung in Wissenschaft und Kunst* (1963), pp. 228–31, and H. Plessner, "Conditio Humana" in *Propyläen Weltgeschichte,* vol. I (1961), pp. 36 f.
[36] Mirgeler, "Erfahrung in der Geschichte", p. 230.
[37] *Ibid.*   [38] *Ibid.*   [39] *Ibid.*

up of unrest. It is in the very nature of the case that under these circumstances a fresh re-appraisal of the problem of the truth of Scripture is called for. It remains, therefore, since for us Scripture is a book which has emerged from within history, to enquire how we should regard this problem of the truth of Scripture, taking into account the general state of the question currently being discussed of the truth to be found in scientific history[40] and in other sciences. To what sort of truth can the history of Israel lay claim, when it is viewed in the perspective of contemporary history writing? For this is preoccupied with presenting a true picture of the history of humanity. What place can Israel lay claim to within the universal history of the development of humanity, now for the first time emerging into view, and in what manner can this be shown to be true? Before an answer can be given to these questions we must call attention to one further attempt at providing a fresh solution to the problem of revelation. For it is precisely from the direction in which this leads that considerable light is thrown on the present state of the problem.

In *Dei Verbum* the question of the truth of Scripture is treated of in various ways. It is particularly striking that with regard to the Old Testament no attempt is made to define more precisely the historical truth of this part of sacred Scripture (ch. IV, art. 14–16). Only with reference to the New Testament is it said that the Church has always firmly upheld the historicity (ch. V, art. 19) of the four gospels. And even here no precise definition of truth is presented as the only possible basis for interpreting the concept of historicity.

Yet there can be no mistaking the fact that the sole reasons for alluding to the truth of Scripture and revelation in *Dei Verbum* are first that the truth of God is being spoken of throughout the

---

[40] On this see also J. Vogt, "Wahrheit in der Geschichtswissenschaft", *Wissenschaft und Weisheit*, pp. 90–102 (with bibliography), R. Wittram, *Das Interesse an der Geschichte* (2nd ed., 1963), pp. 20 ff., and Loretz, *Galilei*, p. 141 f.

document, and second that in ch. III, art. 11 it actually refers *expressis verbis* to the truth of Scripture. Moreover, apart from this passage in ch. III, art. 11 concerning the truth of Scripture, the word 'truth' is central to *Dei Verbum* viewed as a whole.[41] 1. — The revealed truth concerning God and the salvation of mankind is brought to light in Christ (ch. I, art. 2); 2. — The living and true God (ch. I, art. 3), Spirit of truth (ch. I, art. 4); 4. — Belief in the truth of the gospels (ch. I, art. 5); 5. — The gospel is the source of all saving truth (ch. II, art. 7); 6. — Charism of truth (ch. II, art. 8); 7. — Fulness of truth — consummation (ch. II, art. 8); 8. — The Spirit guides into all truth (ch. II, art. 8); 9. — Spirit of truth (ch. II, art. 9); 10. — Truth of God (ch. II, art. 13); 11. — God the true (ch. IV, art. 14); 12. — True word of God (ch. IV, art. 14); 13. — Full of grace and truth (ch. V, art. 17); 14. — Spirit of truth (ch. V, art. 19); 15. — the Spirit guides into all truth (ch. V, art. 20) and 16. — Truth in the mystery of Christ (ch. VI, art. 24).

A distinct question, which must be treated of at a later stage, is that concerning the more precise definition of the concept of truth which recurs throughout *Dei Verbum*.[42]

[41] For an analysis of *Dei Verbum* under this aspect cf. Loretz, *Galilei*, pp. 202 ff.
[42] Cf. p. 52.

CHAPTER TWO

REVELATION AS HISTORY?

W. Pannenberg, R. Rendtorff, U. Wilckens and T. Rendtorff have published a collection of essays under the title *Offenbarung als Geschichte* (Revelation as History).[1] In this they attempt to establish a new definition of the concept of revelation. Since divine revelation was made actual within history, the question of the relationship between revelation and history is of first importance. The precise nature of this mutual relationship has a direct and vital bearing on the question of the truth of the Bible.[2]

W. Pannenberg provides an 'Introduction'[3] in which he prepares for the contributions which are to follow. The question of the meaning of the concept 'revelation' in contemporary work in dogma is first raised, and it is pointed out that the idea is employed in manifold ways. Despite all differences, however, Pannenberg believes it possible to maintain that "a remarkable degree of general agreement does exist on one point, namely that revelation is essentially *self*-revelation on the part of God".[4]

---

[1] *KDB* 1. Here we can only notice in passing that G. Auzou, in his *La Parole de Dieu* (3rd ed., 1963), p. 167, entitles one of his chapters "L'histoire qui est révélation".

[2] L. Alonso-Schökel, *Bib* 46 (1965), p. 378 considers that this and the following chapter maintain only slight contact with the theme of truth in Scripture *("con una periférica tangencia a nuestro tema")*. But this is true only if the inerrancy of the Bible is being discussed from the standpoint of traditional theology.

[3] *KDB* 1, pp. 7–20.   [4] *Ibid.*, pp. 7f.

He goes on to point out that according to current acceptation of the term, "revelation is thought of not as an act by which God gives man information of some matter otherwise concealed from him, but — as Karl Barth puts it — as the 'unveiling of himself' by God".[5] According to this manner of conceiving of revelation, then, the concept is used wholly and solely of the self-disclosure of God, and any idea of supernatural truths being imparted is excluded from it.[6] Pannenberg attempts to show that this manner of conceiving of revelation is a derivation of German idealism: "The 'Enlightenment' had overthrown the earlier concept of revelation maintained by 17th century dogmatic theologians of the orthodox school, according to which revelation was identified with the inspiration of sacred Scripture, and was understood to signify the imparting of supernatural truths otherwise concealed from man. Those who maintained this way of conceiving of revelation were suspected of favouring the obscurantist approach that shunned the light of scientific judgment. Since the beginning of the 19th century this attitude of suspicion and condemnation had relegated the supernatural to the realm of superstition. It was possible to rescue the concept of revelation from this fate only by restricting its content to the *self*-disclosure of God."[7] But whereas Schleiermacher and the younger Schelling still recognize a whole range of self-proclamations on God's part, Hegel introduces a new modification even in this altered view: "Hegel appears to have been the first to introduce the idea of revelation as used strictly of self-disclosure on the part of the Absolute. For it is in his works that it first becomes evident that the self-proclamations of God cannot be otherwise than unique. Hegel in fact regarded the title of 'a religion that is revealed and revealing' as applicable to Christianity alone, not because it contains truths which have been imparted in a supernatural manner, but because, in contrast to all other religions, it is based upon the full

[5] *Ibid.*, p. 8.
[6] *Ibid.*   [7] *Ibid.*

disclosure of the essence of the Absolute as Spirit."[8] According to this view, then, self-revelation is understood in so strict a sense that the idea of any medium of divine revelation whatsoever other than God himself is quite unthinkable, or rather: "Jesus Christ was, in his manhood, the creaturely medium of revelation. As such he was raised up as a medium distinct from God himself. But then he was assumed into union with God. A creaturely medium of revelation that continued to have its own distinct mode of existence, so that the difference between it and God was maintained, would inevitably imply an adulteration, so to say, of the divine light, would introduce an element of inadequacy into the manifestation of God, and so would make the fulness of revelation impossible of achievement."[9]

Pannenberg goes on to emphasize that Karl Barth's idea of revelation is rooted in German idealism, and that Barth merely draws the necessary conclusions from it: *"The idea of revelation as a unique act* follows as a necessary consequence from the restricted idea of God's self-revelation in Barth's presentation too, but with a certain new incisiveness. Those who oppose Barth's idea that the revelation in Christ is the *only* revelation properly so called have apparently never properly adverted to the fact that this idea of revelation as unique is already included in their own restricted conception of revelation as self-revelation. It is precisely in what is special and determinative in the incarnation, death and resurrection of Christ that God is fully revealed. And if this is indeed the case, then God cannot 'also' be revealed in events, situations and persons which are different from these ones. The moment we speak of several revelations we make it impossible to go on thinking of any revelation in the strict sense at all."[10]

---

[8] Cf. Hegel, *Phänomenologie des Geistes* (original edition, 1807), p. 636; Pannenberg, *KDB* 1, p. 9, n. 7, makes further reference to *Phänomenologie des Geistes,* pp. 711 f.; Hegel's *Enzyklopädie,* § 564. Philosophy of religion according to vol. XV of the Jubilee edition of Hegel's works, p. 100, and vol. XVI, pp. 192 ff. [9] *KDB* 1, pp. 8 f.   [10] *Ibid.,* pp. 9 f.

More than other theologians who speak of a plurality of revelations (Troeltsch, Tillich, van der Leeuw — divine power being
made directly 'transparent' through a medium distinct from the
Godhead itself — P. Althaus, E. Brunner — a distinction to be
drawn in terms of the economy of salvation between creational
revelation and salvific revelation) Karl Barth has had, according
to Pannenberg, to recognize that "revelation in the strict sense"
is conceivable only "if the particular medium through which God
is revealed, the particular act by which he manifests himself is
inseparable from his own essence".[11] Pannenberg then continues:
"Karl Barth, with his emphasis on the fact that the concept of
revelation necessarily includes the idea of God's oneness with
Jesus Christ, has recognized this fact more than all contemporary
theologians. The oneness of Jesus with God is oneness in revelation, and as such implies oneness in essence. Hence it follows
that the oneness of Jesus with God in the act of revelation must
lie at the roots of all christological statements concerning the
Godhead of Jesus Christ."[12]

Having established the fact that the idea of God's self-revelation is widely and generally accepted in current theology,
Pannenberg goes on to remind us that the use of this idea as a
theological concept still needs to be justified, and it has not yet
been made clear "how the self-revelation of God has been
accomplished in the concrete".[13] Pannenberg is right in demand-
ing further that "Our way of speaking of the self-revelation of
God, if it is to be established as correct, must in some sense be
supported by biblical witnesses . . . for the biblical writings constitute the fundamental witnesses to those events to which
theology refers us when it speaks of revelation".[14]

But when this line of theological thinking is brought into
confrontation with Scripture, the result is, according to Pannenberg: "that it now appears at first sight that the biblical writings
contain no explicit mention of the self-revelation of God. This

[11] *Ibid.,* p. 10.   [12] *Ibid.,* pp. 10f.   [13] *Ibid.,* p. 11.   [14] *Ibid.,* p. 12.

applies first to the New Testament. In no single passage of the New Testament do the Greek words which are translated 'to reveal' have God as their direct object without further interpositions. God always reveals 'something' or 'someone', never actually himself. The first instance of any such formulation is found in Ignatius (*Magn.* 8, 2). When we examine the Hebrew words represented by the German 'offenbaren' (to reveal) we arrive at a result which does not materially differ from that mentioned above."[15] The manifestations and apparitions of God recorded in the Old Testament can also be regarded as self-disclosures on his part. "But apart from such apparitions, when we examine the actual terms employed as equivalent to 'reveal' we do not come to any solid conclusions which can throw light upon the question of God's self-revelation. This applies especially to the various stories (including those describing how a prophet receives the word), in the narration of which terminology of this kind is employed: in such cases it is always some definite 'matter' that Yahweh imparts, never simply a revelation of 'himself' without further qualification."[16]

As the result of his attempt to discover the theological expression of God's self-revelation in the Scriptures, Pannenberg is forced to record: "It has been made manifest that in terms of the actual expressions used the idea of God's self-revelation has left no mark whatever upon the writings of the Old and New Testaments."[17]

Lest, however, it might appear to be inadequate to confine oneself merely to an investigation of the terms used, Pannenberg puts the question: "But perhaps the area of investigation should be broadened so as to include other aspects besides the merely linguistic ones."[18]. He therefore considers certain examples which, of their very nature, might be expected to include the idea of a direct self-disclosure on the part of God. First he rightly

[15] *Ibid.* [16] *Ibid.*
[17] *Ibid.* [18] *Ibid.*

opposes the views of Karl Barth[19] and H. Vogel[20] by maintaining that the proclamation of the name of God cannot count as a direct self-revelation on his part. The reason is that God makes his name known in the first instance in order that the Israelites may call upon him.[21] It is no less impossible to regard the name 'Jesus Christ' as a concept in which the essence of New Testament revelation is epitomized: "Nothing can be deduced from the decisive importance which this name bears for Christian believers. Here too, moreover, the mere knowledge of the name does not yet of itself imply that full knowledge of the Being to which the name refers that would be the correlative of God's act of self-revelation."[22] The *word of God* is similarly to be regarded: "In the history of biblical tradition this does not bear the significance — except perhaps quite marginally — of a direct self-proclamation of God such as is presupposed in modern 'personalist' theology."[23] The word of God in the Bible "is never applied directly to God himself".[24] Pannenberg is therefore of opinion that "the idea of a direct verbal self-disclosure of God, even when mediated through a revealer, is found in the New Testament only to the extent that unmitigatedly Gnostic ideas on revelation are expressed in it".[25]

Pannenberg also rejects the attempt of W. Elert[26] to take the proclamation of the *law* at Sinai and of the gospel in the New Testament as acts of direct self-revelation by God, on the grounds that the proclamation of the laws presupposes a prior revelation which has already been given.[27]

Pannenberg concludes his consideration concerning the theory of the self-revelation of God with the negative statement

---

[19] K. Barth, *Kirchliche Dogmatik* I/1 (1952), pp. 334 ff., E. T.: *Church Dogmatics,* ed. by G. W. Bromiley and T. F. Torrance, vol. I, part I (1949).

[20] H. Vogel, *Gott in Christo* (2nd ed., 1952), pp. 162 ff.

[21] *KDB* 1, p. 13.   [22] *Ibid.*   [23] *Ibid.*   [24] *Ibid.*

[25] *Ibid.,* p. 14. Pannenberg mentions Heb 1:2; Jn 1:1 ff.

[26] W. Elert, *Der christliche Glaube* (3rd ed., 1956), § 23, pp. 138 ff.

[27] *KDB* 1, p. 15.

that so far no such self-revelation has been established, and at the same time he goes on to point out that the evidence of Yahweh's divinity is to be found in his deeds in history: "In closing it must be stated that the theory of a direct self-revelation of God, as maintained by theologians, cannot be justified either in terms of the words equivalent to 'to reveal' in the original languages of the Bible, or in terms of the three conceptual fields referred to here (Proclamation of the name, word of God and law), to which some such significance has been ascribed. Even in cases in which other ideas, such as that of Yahweh's glory, imply the idea of direct self-disclosure as their origin, still these ideas have been absorbed into the traditions of the Old Testament. The viewpoint from which they can be so absorbed is one which is decisive for Israel, namely that the basic evidence for Yahweh's divinity is to be found in his deeds in history. The idea which we encounter here corresponds to the actual facts: instead of a direct self-revelation by God we find an indirect self-revelation by him as he is reflected in his acts in history. His words and actions viewed as a whole, that is as the history created by Yahweh, show us indirectly who he is. We should notice the significance which this indirect self-disclosure by God bears for the entire Israelite apocalyptic and pre-Christian history of tradition. It is only in the light of this that the negative statements which assert that the idea of a direct self-revelation by God is absent, or which relegate it to the background, acquire their full relevance and importance."[28]

Since Pannenberg speaks of an "indirect self-revelation of God as reflected in his active intervention in history",[29] he has to provide some further elucidation of this idea. As his starting-point for this further elucidation he takes the relation of indirect to direct communication. The criterion for distinguishing between direct and indirect communication is "not the directness or indirectness of the act of communication itself, but the question

[28] *Ibid.,* pp. 15 f.
[29] *Ibid.,* p. 16.

of whether the *matter communicated* does or does not coincide with *the object for the attainment of which* it is communicated".[30]

Thus whereas revelation is direct when it has "God himself as its immediate subject-matter",[31] the distinguishing characteristic of *indirect* revelation "is that God is not the *immediate* object revealed".[32] Every intervention of God throws light upon this 'selfhood' of his, but does not fully reveal him: "Each individual event, regarded as an act of God, throws light upon the nature of God, but only fragmentarily. God is always performing many other acts, while still remaining invisible himself, and these lead our vision back to him as their performer. On this basis no single activity of his seems able to reveal him. On the contrary, to conceive of a single divine activity, taken in isolation, as *the* revelation of God leads to a distorted view, to idolatry."[33]

This argument has the effect of excluding the theory that every individual act of God is revelation. For if such a theory were correct there would be innumerable revelations in nature and history, and it would no longer be possible to speak of any self-revelation on God's part. These considerations lead Pannenberg to conclude that "the only valid course, therefore, is to take God's activity as a whole as divine revelation — and when it is the unique God that is in question this can only mean all that takes place considered as a whole. From this point two courses are open to us. If we take the whole of reality, with its static and unchangeable interrelationships (i. e. considered as 'cosmos') as an indirect communication of what the true God is, then we are following the line of Greek philosophy, and considering the problem of God from the standpoint of 'natural theology'. If, on that other hand, we think of the whole of reality as time-conditioned and subject to change — in other words as history, and then regard this as the self-communication of God, then we find

---

[30] *Ibid.*
[31] *Ibid.*, p. 17.
[32] *Ibid.*   [33] *Ibid.*

ourselves on the course marked out by German idealistic thinking from Lessing and Herder onwards."[34]

According to Pannenberg[35] it was Schleiermacher[36] who first attracted notice in 1799 by "the explicit assertion that history as a whole is God's revelation, and that as such it constitutes the special matter with which the Christian religion, as distinct from all other religions, is concerned". In 1802 Schelling formulated the idea as a principle,[37] and "Hegel systematically carried through the conception of universal history as the indirect self-revelation of God, at the same time elucidating the concept of self-revelation".[38] In this respect the later Schelling took up Hegel's theory again.[39]

Against this conception, however, objections have been raised. "First, if it is only history as a whole that constitutes the revelation of God, how then can one particular event in history — the fate of Jesus — have an absolute significance as divine revelation?"[40] This question led D. F. Strauss[41] to the theory that the fulness of an idea is not manifested in an individual case, but first appears in the development of a group or class. Since *in concreto* Strauss is thinking of the idea of the union of God and man, what he means here is that this applies not to the single individual, Jesus, but to mankind as an emergent group; "but since the Hegelian concept of the self-revelation of God . . . is closely connected with the idea of the 'God-man' union of the Incarnation — is indeed based upon this idea — Strauss is logically consistent when in his teaching on faith he reduces the concept of revelation to the idea of

---

[34] *Ibid.,* pp. 17 f. [35] *Ibid.,* p. 18.

[36] Schleiermacher, *Über die Religion* (1799), pp. 293 f.

[37] K. F. A. Schelling, the ninth section of his lecture on the method of academic study in M. Schröter, ed., *Werke,* vol. III (1958), pp. 318–27.

[38] *KDB* 1, p. 18.

[39] W. Schulz, *Die Vollendung des deutschen Idealismus in der Spätphilosophie Schellings* (1955), pp. 259–70.

[40] *KDB* 1, p. 18.

[41] D. F. Strauss, *Das Leben Jesu,* vol. II (3rd ed., 1839), pp. 778 f.

mankind as an emergent group."[42] So, far from regarding Strauss' thought as a final rounding off of the Hegelian propositions, Pannenberg sees it as "a radical misunderstanding of Hegel".[43] According to Pannenberg the theory propounded by Strauss was followed by a fourth reaction: "The objection might have been raised against Strauss on dogmatic grounds that it is not the concept of revelation which can be established from an idea of the Incarnation, but vice versa, the 'God-man' union in Jesus Christ which is deducible from the fact of the revelation of God in him, and the basis for this is to be sought elsewhere. Instead of opposing Strauss' theory along these lines, however, not only Kirkegaard, but the entire theology of the period after Strauss reacted by asserting a fresh cleavage between the event of salvation and the history of the universe, depending in this on the tradition of supernaturalism."[44]

A further objection which, so Pannenberg contends, can be raised against the Hegelian conception of revelation can be stated as follows: " . . . if history as a whole is to be regarded as revelation, then further advances in revelation must take place, beyond those which took place in Jesus Christ."[45]

Still according to Pannenberg, the 19th century thinker R. Rothe introduced a further significant development in the theology of the idea of revelation: "the effects of German idealism on Rothe appear in the fact that he too conceives of revelation as history, as the interconnection of events. Rothe reacted both against the idea of 'an interior miracle' put forward by the earlier teaching on inspiration, and against Schleiermacher's transformation of the doctrine of inspiration, in which he restricts it to the interior attitude of a devout spirit and reduces it to personal inspiration. Rothe, on the other hand, insisted that Scripture presents the self-revelation of God as 'a continuously inter-

---

[42] *KDB* 1, p. 18; D. F. Strauss, *Die christliche Glaubenslehre,* vol. I (1840), pp. 274 ff.
[43] *KDB* 1, p. 18. [44] *Ibid.,* pp. 18 f. [45] *Ibid.,* p. 19.

connected series of miraculous events in history and manipulations of history'.[46] Thus Rothe no longer regarded history as a whole as the revelation of God, but only the 'supernatural history' recorded in biblical tradition.[47] Here, in other words, historical events are treated of which are 'of such a nature that they can only be explained by having recourse to the idea of God, since they cannot be derived from worldly causes'.[48] This meant that revelation was once more confined to the sphere of specifically biblical history, but, as with Hoffmann's theory of salvation history, Rothe had come suspiciously close to the old supernaturalism, even though he himself had not, in principle, postulated any cleavage between sacred and profane history."[49]

At the end of his 'introduction' Pannenberg comes to the following conclusion: "The idea of an indirect self-revelation of God through the history which he himself has brought into being is therefore not new. Like the idea that revelation consists exclusively of self-revelation, it has its origin, from the standpoint of the history of ideas, in German idealism. Yet, as I have indicated, it is hedged about with a whole series of difficulties. An individual act of God, an individual event, can indeed throw an indirect light upon its originator, but it cannot constitute a full revelation of the one God. On the other hand, it is not within our power to view history as a whole, as though it were no longer open to further development. But even if we could do this, the nature of universal history as limitless, and its relentless onward progress, make it seemingly impossible for any one individual event to have an absolute significance such as that which Christian faith finds in the fate of Christ."[50]

The investigations which follow, into the ways in which the Old and New Testaments understand revelation, are intended to establish whether the Bible affords us any evidence on which to

[46] A. Rothe, *Zur Dogmatik* (1863), p. 59.
[47] *Ibid.,* p. 67.   [48] *Ibid.,* p. 66.
[49] *KDB* 1, p. 19.   [50] *Ibid.,* p. 20.

base a conception of the indirect self-revelation of God such as will solve the difficulties mentioned above.

The next essay in the symposium is an investigation of R. Rendtorff's, entitled 'The Ways in which Revelation was Conceived of in Ancient Israel'.[51] Having devoted a few brief lines to pointing out the unsatisfying nature of such statements as current theology has offered with regard to revelation in the Old Testament, this author first treats of revelation terminology in the Old Testament.[52] As used in the Old Testament the verb *gālāh* (ἀποκαλύπτειν) — 'reveal, uncover, unveil' — is not a theological term with a single unified concept underlying it. For this reason it is not suitable as a point of departure for the investigation.[53] In no passage is there any mention of a self-revelation of God in the sense in which the term is employed in current theology. All that is said is that Yahweh causes himself to be seen or announces himself.[54]

According to Rendtorff the earliest and most original usage to be met with is that in which the deity is said to 'cause himself to be seen' *(nir'āh)*. Such apparitions of God are originally connected with a particular *place* (Ex 3). According to Rendtorff in the context of cult aetiology the *nifal* form of *rā'āh* has the following history behind it: "The Yahwist uses it several times to express Yahweh's self-manifestation in an extremely summary form: the deity appears, and in response to this the man who has been favoured with this apparition builds an altar."[55] (Gen 12:6f.; 26:24f.; cf. Gen 17:1b, 3, 22b.) In Genesis 35:9ff. it is only the words of God that still continue to be presented according to this pattern, and the separation from a place of cult has been accomplished. "The narrative as a whole survives only to provide a setting of suitable solemnity for the words which God speaks. But above all emphasis no longer continues to be laid on the visual apparition of Yahweh. Thus there is no direct line here, leading from the linguistic usage associated with cult aetiology to

---

[51] *Ibid.,* pp. 21–41.   [52] *Ibid.,* pp. 23ff.
[53] *Ibid.,* p. 23.   [54] *Ibid.,* p. 23.   [55] *Ibid.,* pp. 23f.

the concept of a theophany of Yahweh. Nowhere in the Old Testament is the concept expressed by *nir'āh* used of a cultic theophany."[56] The development of the concept expressed by *nir'āh* takes another direction, for it is connected with the pronouncement of a *promise by God* (Gen 12:7 — Promise of possession of the land; Gen 26:24 — Promise of offspring; Ex 3 — Promise of the exodus from Egypt). More and more the emphasis is transferred from the sensible apparition of Yahweh to the announcement of what he is to perform (cf. Gen 26:2f.; Judges 6:12ff.; 13:3ff.; 1 Kings 3:5ff.; 9:2ff.).[57] In the course of time the concept of Yahweh causing himself to be seen is regarded as inappropriate and thrust into the background, with the result that 'to appear' *(nir'āh)* comes to be rivalled by the more favoured term *nôda'*, 'to let oneself be known' (cf. Ex 6:3). With the advent of Moses the preliminary stages in which Yahweh *appears* are left behind, and Yahweh now allows himself 'to be known *as himself*',[58] in that he imparts his name.

Before Rendtorff goes on to explain the significance of the statement that Yahweh allows himself to be known by his name, he has something more to say about the passages which speak of Yahweh being made known by reason of his deeds (pp. 25ff.). In many passages it is stated that Yahweh himself becomes visible in his mighty deeds of salvation, both past and future. Another way in which Yahweh appears is through the medium of his *kabôd* — 'glory'. According to Rendtorff a radical transformation of Canaanite ideas is apparent in Isaiah 6:3 ('Holy, holy, holy is Yahweh Sabaoth'; what fills the whole earth is his *kabôd*). For now the *kabôd* of the God-king no longer fills heaven alone, but earth also. "As the Israelite mind understands it, the decisive characteristic in the nature of God is precisely his giving of himself to the world."[59] According to Psalm 97 and Deutero-Isaiah the manifestation of his glory signifies the "evident fulfilment of his

56 *Ibid.*, p. 24.   57 *Ibid.*, p. 25, n. 15.
58 *Ibid.*, p. 25.   59 *Ibid.*, p. 28.

power".[60] According to the Priestly tradition, on the other hand, the *kabôd* of Yahweh appears in order to announce an impending demonstration of God's power.[61] In a second group of passages (Ex 24:15ff.; 25ff.; 40:34f.; Lev 9:23f.) the *kabôd* of Yahweh appears at the inauguration of the cult. Ezekiel too stands in this same tradition, only in his writings it is adapted to the special situation of the exilic period. "The continuity of the presence of Yahweh in the cultic context of the Jerusalem temple is interrupted; Yahweh is present to his authentic community in the exile until the time when the cult of the temple is finally restored."[62]

Basing himself on the works of W. Zimmerli,[63] Rendtorff goes on to consider "the formula *'anî YHWH* as an expression particularly pregnant in meaning"[64] for our understanding of Yahweh's self-disclosure, the manner in which he makes himself known *(yada')*. With Zimmerli Rendtorff comes down in favour of the rendering 'I am Yahweh' for *'anî YHWH,* so that his translation reads 'I am Yahweh, your God' and not 'I, Yahweh, am your God' or its equivalent. By being combined with the verb *yada'* the formula *'anî YHWH* becomes relevant in the context of revelation and the way in which it is imparted. In fact it acquires special relevance by reason of its frequent occurrence in the phrase *'yada' kî 'anî YHWH,* 'to know that I am Yahweh'. The implication of this formula is that knowledge of Yahweh can be gained only from his actions in history. "From a survey of the biblical evidence, commencing with the pentateuchal sources, passing on from there to the narrative of the prophets in 1 Kings 20, and beyond this again to the 'post-Ezekiel' tradition, it appears that there is no difference whatever in the terms employed.

---

[60] *Ibid.,* p. 29.   [61] *Ibid.,* p. 30.   [62] *Ibid.,* p. 31.

[63] W. Zimmerli, "Ich bin Jahwe" in *Geschichte und Altes Testament, Festschrift A. Alt* (1953), pp. 179–209; id., *Erkenntnis Gottes nach dem Buche Ezechiel* (1954); id., "Das Wort des göttlichen Selbsterweises (Erweiswort), eine prophetische Gattung" in *Mélanges Bibliques rédigés en l'honneur d'André Robert* (1957), pp. 154–64.

[64] *KDB* 1, p. 32.

In passages in which knowing Yahweh is expressly mentioned it is connected with his manifestation of himself in history."[65] It is seeing and experiencing Yahweh's deeds that brings knowledge of his incomparable sublimity and his uniqueness: " 'To you it was shown, that you might know that the Lord is God; there is no other besides him' (Deut 4:35; cf. 37–40). This entire history, therefore, has the aim of causing Yahweh to be known, bringing knowledge of the fact that he alone is God and he alone has power."[66]

The formula is often combined with a reference to the future. Knowledge of Yahweh will be awakened by future events. In the prophetic tradition in particular the 'knowledge' formula is connected with events which have still to take place. Then with Ezekiel a change comes; the 'knowledge' formula is no longer associated with particular events in history, as in the earlier prophetic tradition, but to an overwhelming extent with the 'judgment' oracles. The same is also true of Deutero-Isaiah. The assertion that Yahweh will be known is referred entirely to his manifestation of himself, which is still awaited as a future event. Yahweh's manifestation of himself in history is more and more emphatically assigned to the realm of future expectation.

In conclusion Rendtorff emphasizes the point that "throughout the entire history of the 'knowledge' formula it is stated again and again that not only Israel, but precisely the other peoples too are to know Yahweh in his divinity".[67] From Yahweh's deeds the whole world is to derive knowledge of himself (cf. Ps. 98:2f.; Is 40:5). The events of the history in which God is at work are of fundamental importance "because in them God manifests himself as himself. This, of course, is to be known in the present, and in fact by him who actually sees and experiences the events in question. The all-essential point, therefore, for that understanding of revelation which is basic to our present consideration is to take the event itself as our point of departure, to allow it, without

---

[65] *Ibid.,* p. 35.   [66] *Ibid.,* p. 36.   [67] *Ibid.,* p. 38.

restriction, to have its full weight as an event, and, on the part of the man concerned, to keep in view how he stands in relation to this event as he recognizes or fails to recognize in it the self-manifestation of God."[68]

Finally Rendtorff returns once more to the problem of how event and word are related to each other, for "the 'knowledge' formula is always found on the lips of a speaker specially authorized by Yahweh".[69] Rendtorff attributes to the word, however, only an "essential share in the event of revelation",[70] for the prophetic oracle is not as such to be taken as revelation. "For this is not the self-manifestation of Yahweh at all; rather it anticipates it or refers back to it again and again. Knowledge is not engendered by the oracle taken in isolation, but only by the event announced in the oracle taken in its historical context."[71] According to the teaching of the Old Testament, however, it is the event itself which is to "engender knowledge of Yahweh in him who sees it and understands it in its context as an act of Yahweh".[72] Especially with regard to the actions which Yahweh performs before the peoples Rendtorff argues that "any connection between revelation and prophetic oracle appears excluded from the outset".[73]

Ancient Israel knows Yahweh in his historical deeds, in which he "manifests himself as himself".[74] In the course of time the Old Testament references to the revelation of Yahweh point more and more exclusively to the future, and "after the political catastrophe of 587 B.C. the final self-manifestation of Yahweh is awaited as the decisive event of the future".[75] The experiences of history have led Israel to an awareness of the fact that the final and definitive revelation of Yahweh has still to take place.

In his contribution, 'The Understanding of Revelation in the History of Early Christianity',[76] U. Wilckens attempts to amplify

---

[68] *Ibid.,* p. 39.   [69] *Ibid.,* p. 40.   [70] *Ibid.*
[71] *Ibid.*   [72] *Ibid.*   [73] *Ibid.*
[74] *Ibid.*   [75] *Ibid.*   [76] *Ibid.,* pp. 42–90.

and complement the biblical concept of revelation on the basis of the New Testament. At the end of his extremely full investigation Wilckens too comes to the conclusion that revelation is imparted through events. "Although the witnesses of early Christianity are so disparate in other respects, they all concur in the judgment that revelation in the theological sense here taken to be fundamental takes place solely in the event of the return from the dead of the crucified Jesus of Nazareth, in which God permitted the new aeon to commence."[77]

Extending the argument beyond what has hitherto been said W. Pannenberg then puts forward seven "dogmatic theses on the doctrine of revelation".[78]

His first thesis runs as follows: 'According to the biblical evidence the self-revelation of God was accomplished not directly in the form of some kind of theophany, but indirectly through God's acts in history.'[79] Here Pannenberg is recapitulating what has been said in the two preceding essays. From this he passes on to his second thesis: 'Revelation takes place not at the beginning of this revelatory history but at its end.'[80] According to Pannenberg the association of revelation with the end of history is most closely connected with its indirectness. This is the fundamental presupposition: only when the events of history have taken place "can the divinity of God be recognized in them. Thus the 'coming to light' of revelation is assigned a place at the end of history because of its nature as indirect."[81] Then in apocalyptic it is expressly stated that only at the end of all that is to take place will Yahweh finally and definitively reveal himself as the one and unique God. Since, as Pannenberg argues, revelation moves closer and closer towards its end as history unfolds, at the beginning of Israel's history she must not be artificially isolated from the world about her "by maintaining the idea of a supernatural revelation taking place in the context of her own origins".[82] But

---

[77] *Ibid.,* p. 87.   [78] *Ibid.,* pp. 91–114.   [79] *Ibid.,* p. 91.
[80] *Ibid.,* p. 95.   [81] *Ibid.,* p. 96.   [82] *Ibid.,* p. 97.

since in the fate of Jesus the end of all history has been anticipated, the God of Israel has manifested himself in him as the one true God. Recognizing that this event has a universal character, Pannenberg can pass on to his next thesis: 'In contrast to particular apparitions of the deity, revelation in history is open to anyone who has eyes to see. It has a universal character.'[83] In the exposition of this thesis emphasis is laid upon this open and public character of revelation, the fact that the events which are the vehicle of revelation are able to be known by all. Anyone who is not blind can see that God has revealed himself.

The next (fourth) thesis[84] is concerned with the question, 'To what extent is God revealed in the history of Israel and in Jesus of Nazareth?' 'The universal revelation of the divinity of God is not yet made actual in the history of Israel, but only in what befell Jesus of Nazareth inasmuch as in this the end of all history has taken place by anticipation.'[85] In the New Testament we find for the first time that the end of the world is not merely looked forward to, as in the apocalyptic writings, but has actually taken place by anticipation. "For the destiny which awaits all men, namely the raising of the dead to life, has actually taken place in him."[86] No one, however, can overlook or eliminate the message of this self-manifestation of God, here expressed in individual terms, yet pointing on to a future that is unimaginable, so that this revelation of God in Christ provides no basis for a "rationalistically comprehensive knowledge"[87] of God. In the fate undergone by Jesus Christ God reveals himself as the triune God, and thereby communicates his own nature. In this way the doctrine of the Trinity gives expression to "the idea of God as contained in a revelation that has taken place in history".[88] Since the revelation of God in the event of Christ anticipates the end of history, this cannot "be surpassed by any subsequent event,

---

[83] *Ibid.*, p. 98.   [84] *Ibid.*, pp. 103–106.
[85] *Ibid.*, p. 103.   [86] *Ibid.*, p. 104.
[87] *Ibid.*, p. 105.   [88] *Ibid.*

and continues always to transcend all our powers of apprehension also".[89]

The fifth thesis runs: 'It is not as an isolated event that what befell Christ reveals the divinity of the God of Israel, but only insofar as this constitutes an element in the history of God with Israel.'[90] Since the prophetic and apocalyptic expectation of the end represents a decisive factor in determining the form of Jesus' coming and his fate, it can be understood from this point of view that his Resurrection is the divine authentication of the claim to omnipotence which he made in his pre-Easter mission. The resurrection of the dead expected by the apocalyptists, which has already taken place in Christ, attests the fact that in him the end has already begun, and therefore that in him God is revealed.

Pannenberg formulates his penultimate (6th) thesis in the following terms: 'The universality of God's eschatological self-manifestation finds expression in the development of non-Jewish ideas of revelation in the Gentile Christian Church.'[91] In the course of developing this thesis Pannenberg lays down that Gnostic forms of expression were laid under contribution by Christian preachers in order that by these means the universality of the eschatological self-manifestation of God in the fate of Jesus could be preached to Gentile Christians also.

The last of Pannenberg's theses is formulated as follows: 'The word is related to revelation as prediction, as command, as instruction.'[92] Since in the course of the foregoing explanations he has spoken only of history, whereas the word in the Old and New Testaments speaks of the historical events, Pannenberg seeks to justify his position from this point of view also. The three points which he considers chief in importance regarding the question of how word and revelation are related are: 1. The word of God as promise — the prophetic word acquires the force of a self-manifestation of Yahweh only by being fulfilled. 2. The word

[89] *Ibid.*, p. 106.   [90] *Ibid.*, p. 107.
[91] *Ibid.*, p. 109.   [92] *Ibid.*, p. 112.

of God as command — "Law and commandment are the outcome of the divine self-manifestation; they are not of themselves revelatory in character, except to the extent that the very fact of Yahweh laying down what is right, like the rest of his acts, shows indirectly who he is."[93] 3. The word of God as *kerygma* (New Testament) — "the word of the *kerygma* is precisely not, of itself, the act of revelation proper, it is rather an element in this act of revelation, in that it informs or instructs men concerning the eschatological event which is, in itself, the sufficient self-manifestation of God. For this self-manifestation demands public proclamation, and it is by being so proclaimed that it finds expression everywhere."[94]

The expositions which have been reviewed here, of W. Pannenberg, R. Rendtorff and U. Wilckens[95] enable us to recognize this much, that revelation is to be understood as history. But a question which still remains at the end of this survey is 'What is the basis for this definition of revelation as history?' What concept of truth has here been presupposed, without being expressed, so that at the end the revelation of God in history can be designated as something open to the clear light of day?

This view of how truth should be defined belongs to the realm of Western metaphysics, and not to the Bible. It is closer to Descartes's definition of truth *Illud omne, quod valde clare et distincte percipitur verum est* (*Med.* III), and is dependent upon the philosophy associated with him.[96] For the explanation of truth here is

---

[93] *Ibid.,* p. 113.   [94] *Ibid.,* p. 114.

[95] T. Rendtorff, "Das Offenbarungsproblem im Kirchenbegriff", *ibid.,* pp. 115–31. This final contribution to the symposium requires no special treatment in the present context.

[96] On the question of truth according to Descartes, Hegel and Nietzsche cf. M. Heidegger, *Nietzsche,* vol. I (1961), pp. 495–516, 616–48; *ibid.,* vol. II, pp. 173–99, 421–9. The characteristics of clarity and certainty are defined by Descartes as follows: "Claram voco illam (ideam) quae menti attendenti praesens et aperta est . . .", *Principia Philosophiae* I, ed. by C. Adam and P. Tannery, *Œuvres de Descartes,* vol. VIII (1905), 22:3–4. "Distinctam autem

decidedly subjective. He who boldly engages his reason appre-
hends the truth, and the voluntary blindness of the unwilling
only signifies "that they will have to be brought to reason in
order that they may perceive rightly".[97] It is not only on the
Protestant side that this influence of the thought of the new era,
so strongly influenced as it is by R. Descartes, makes itself felt. In
Catholic circles the influence of the Cartesian concept of truth is
apparent chiefly in the connection of the concept of the inerrancy
of Scripture with that of 'certainty'. In the more detailed expositions of the inerrancy of the Bible it is said to have infallible
certainty.[98]

illam quae, cum clara sit, ab omnibus aliis ita seiuncta est et praecisa, ut nihil
plane aliud, quam quod clarum est, in se contineat", *ibid.*, 22:6–9. On this
H. Blumenberg, "Paradigmen zu einer Metaphorologie", *Archiv für Begriffsgeschichte* 6 (1960), comments: "The dependence on the Stoic theory of knowledge and on their ideal, the 'cateleptic' concept, is unmistakable but as yet
insufficiently explained." On the Stoic 'apprehending concept' (καταληπτική
φαντασία, κατάληψις) see Blumenberg, *ibid.*, p. 15.

[97] Pannenberg, *KDB* 1, p. 100.

[98] Cf. for example A. Bea, *LTK*, V, col. 706; extensive discussion in Loretz,
Galilei, pp. 43 ff., 186, n. 7.

CHAPTER THREE

OVER-PREOCCUPATION WITH HISTORY?

The natural outcome of the works briefly reviewed in the previous chapter is to give a central place to the historical event. The only self-revelation of God regarded as possible is an indirect one, through God's intervention in history.[1] Right from the outset this approach produces tensions in relation to Scripture itself, for this, as the word of God, is intended to impart revelation as of itself. As the document of revelation it stands on its own feet; it has not hitherto been understood as a mere appendage to the historical interventions of God, and is not so considered now. The upholders of the thesis 'revelation as history' have seen that this element in their conception of revelation gives cause for surprise, and have therefore attempted also to relegate the word to what is, at most, a peripheral place in their scheme.[2] The question is, however, whether the conception of 'revelation as history' as set forth above does not involve an exaggerated emphasis on history at the expense of the word.

W. Zimmerli has come out as an opponent of the interpretation of Old Testament revelation maintained by Rendtorff and (a point which is especially worthy of note) has brought into the discussion those statements in the Old Testament for which R. Rendtorff's explanations are too cursory or too one-sided.[3] While agreeing

---

[1] Cf. *KDB* 1, p. 91.   [2] Cf. *ibid.,* pp. 40, 112–14.

[3] W. Zimmerli, "'Offenbarung' im Alten Testament", *EvTh* 22 (1962), pp. 15–31.

with R. Rendtorff in many respects, though not without occasional reservations,[4] he has the strongest possible reservations to express with regard to Rendtorff's general interpretation of the formula *'anokî YHWH,* 'I am Yahweh (your God)'.[5] Whereas for Rendtorff the name Yahweh is a pregnant expression of God's claim to power, Zimmerli holds firmly to the opinion that this name imports something more, "namely the making present unmistakably and once and for all of God as *person* veiled in mystery — it is this that is expressed in the name".[6] According to Zimmerli the event in which God reveals himself by disclosing his name carries a double connotation: "1. A sovereign freedom. Initially only I myself can call myself by name; no-one obtains it from me by outwitting me if I myself do not reveal it to him. Thus God's presentation of himself takes the form of an assertion that can only be uttered by him to others — never the other way round. The statement 'I am Yahweh' is on a different plane from the statement 'You are Yahweh', the latter being possible only as an echo of the former. It is impossible to reverse this order of dependence. In the statement 'I am Yahweh', as the very manner in which the sentence is constructed shows, 'I' remains the subject. 'I' is the source from which the utterance proceeds. To this first point a second must be added: 2. As a form of self-presentation the name gives expression to the mystery of the person 'I'; it is not a mere cypher, standing for the power of God, as might appear from Rendtorff's exposition of this statement of Yahweh in the first person. Because it has this force it is radically different from any statement purporting to describe realities in the factual order."[7] Thus Zimmerli feels compelled to oppose Rendtorff on the grounds that in his interpretation of the formula 'I am Yahweh' as used by Deutero-Isaiah he has failed to discern the element of uniqueness in it. For he connects it mainly with the majesty of Yahweh and hence overlooks the fact that in Yahweh's utterance of his own proper name here (cf. especially Is. 48, 12) it is what

---

[4] *Ibid.,* pp. 15 ff.   [5] *Ibid.,* pp. 18 ff.   [6] *Ibid.,* p. 21.   [7] *Ibid.*

is "inalienable, individual, personal"[8] in Yahweh's own self that is being expressed. According to Zimmerli Rendtorff "constantly under-estimates the presentation of *self* involved in the utterance of the name, and fails to realize the importance of the fact that so much emphasis is laid upon the promulgation of the name, even in the case of the 'you shall know . . .' formulations".[9] This leads Rendtorff to questionable conclusions.

Thus, as Zimmerli appositely expresses it, for Rendtorff "history emerges as something with an unique and absolute value, sufficient to itself, so that it has no need of illumination by the prophetic word",[10] that is, as the revelation of God proper. Against this Zimmerli feels compelled to observe that this thrusting aside of the prophetic word represents a line of argument which is peculiar to a degree, and one "which quite clearly cannot possibly be in accordance with the real nature of the Old Testament".[11] For, as Zimmerli goes on to remark, Yahweh's intervention in the history of Israel took the form of proclaiming his name and standing by the word which he had spoken (cf. Pharaoh before Moses; 1 Kings 20). Israel is also called to bear witness to the name of Yahweh.[12] Furthermore, Yahweh demonstrates his divine nature (especially in Deutero-Isaiah) by predicting what is to come. Thus "to isolate the history caused by Yahweh from the word sent by Yahweh beforehand . . . is, precisely in the case of Deutero-Isaiah, a procedure which is exegetically untenable"[13] (cf. Is 40:8; 55:10f.). The word of Yahweh already contains in itself the force of "an event that sets the world and history in motion".[14]

In drawing all these points to a conclusion Zimmerli feels compelled, in view of the Old Testament passages, to take up the following position: "All things considered it is a truly amazing undertaking, and one which it is impossible to reconcile with the evidence of the Old Testament, to isolate history from the

[8] *Ibid.*   [9] *Ibid.*, p. 23.   [10] *Ibid.*, p. 24.
[11] *Ibid.*   [12] *Ibid.*, pp. 24 f.   [13] *Ibid.*, p. 25.   [14] *Ibid.*

prophetic word and to ascribe to that word only a completely secondary and incidental role, though certainly this role then demands some kind of further discussion. History is the realization of the word, the fulfilment of prophecy. But central to prophecy is the invocation of Yahweh's name. Israel has been empowered to make this invocation in virtue of the fact that Yahweh has 'called this, his name, upon her', and has thereby affirmed his claim to this people as his own possession. The act by which Yahweh has done this is of fundamental significance; it constitutes a presentation of himself in his divinity which certainly now appears quite unique in character."[15]

Rendtorff, then, regards only the manifestations of God's power in history as revelation, and refuses to allow the word and the name to carry their full significance. In contrast to this Zimmerli is of opinion that this "conception of history as a medium (albeit one which even today has not yet been fully revealed as such), in which God is present as in his revelation proper"[16] is clearly contradicted by the entire Old Testament understanding of history. "As conceived of here history is always an instrument, created and freely manipulated by God. It does not bear an intelligible meaning somehow hidden within itself, to which man can have access in virtue of his interpretative powers. But what is indeed true is that God can, so to say, bring history to life, make it 'speak to' man; and he does this by raising up a prophet who 'calls Yahweh's name upon' the relevant historical event."[17]

Zimmerli, therefore, refuses to ascribe "to history an ultimate value which, so far as the Old Testament is concerned, it does not in reality possess, however deep the meaning may be which, as that in which the knowledge of God is located, it does undoubtedly bear".[18] The history of the Old Testament derives its form from a single fundamental fact, namely that in the course of the unique and astonishing historical event of being liberated under

[15] *Ibid.*, pp. 25 f.   [16] *Ibid.*, p. 28.   [17] *Ibid.*, pp. 28 f.   [18] *Ibid.*, p. 29.

Moses' leadership Israel experienced the summons of Yahweh, and this summons was proclaimed to her in that historical event.[19] This summons of God, therefore, dominates the history of Israel as a whole and gives the faith of Israel its special character. "Israel's faith in her own historical survival is rooted not in some single all-embracing meaning contained in her history, which she understands ever more deeply, but in the faithfulness of Yahweh who will not be untrue to his word and will not abandon that which he has made his own, but will rather continue to treat Israel as his people in the present and in the future 'for the sake of his name' which has been 'called upon' her."[20]

Zimmerli's criticism of Rendtorff's interpretation of the Old Testament understanding of revelation is sharp, and he declares unequivocally that what Rendtorff says is inadmissible. But for all their sharpness it may be allowed that the criticisms he makes are justified.[21] Zimmerli avoids the pitfall of applying any previously formed theory to the relevant Old Testament passages. The extent to which Zimmerli's observations need to be supplemented, however, will be explained in the next chapter.[22]

But if the identification of revelation with the historical manifestations of God's power in the Old Testament is at variance with the facts, then a further question immediately presents

---

[19] *Ibid.,* p. 30.   [20] *Ibid.,* p. 31.

[21] Rendtorff has replied to Zimmerli's objections in his article, "Geschichte und Wort im Alten Testament", *EvTh* 22 (1962), pp. 621–49. In my opinion Rendtorff recognizes the force of Zimmerli's attack, albeit unwillingly, in that he too now works out the meaning of the word in the Old Testament. But if Rendtorff considers that Zimmerli has misunderstood him, and that he has himself perceived the significance of the word from the first, then it must be said that he interprets himself too benignly and that he shows too great a confidence in his own power to interpret correctly. Rendtorff's oberservations on the way in which Zimmerli treats of the name 'Yahweh' are justified (cf. Rendtorff, *art. cit.,* p. 627 n. 16). For a criticism of Rendtorff see further G. Klein, "Offenbarung als Geschichte? Marginalien zu einem theologischen Programm", *Monatschrift für Pastoraltheologie* 51 (1962), pp. 68 ff.

[22] Cf. pp. 53 ff.

itself. In the New Testament, in which Old Testament traditions are, in many respects, carried further, can a concept of revelation be established according to which "the . . . only revelation is that contained in the event of the return from the dead of the crucified Jesus of Nazareth, in whom God caused the new aeon to commence"?[23]

It can be taken as certain that in the New Testament too God reveals himself in what Jesus did and what befell him. This much is quite incontestable. But it would be exaggerated and one-sided to deny that in the New Testament God also makes himself known by his word. Thus for instance according to the Johannine gospel the Son testifies by his words to 'what he has seen and heard' (directly) (Jn 3: 32).[24] The words of Jesus that demand the response of faith, no less than his actual deeds (miracles), are included among the works which he accomplishes, and through which at the same time the Father bears witness to him (cf. Jn 8: 28; 14: 10; 15: 22–24).[25]

Now the Johannine gospel is far from standing alone among the writings of the New Testament in the insight it affords into how Jesus' deed is related to his word. In the other writings too the words which God speaks to man are regarded as an essential part of his action upon him. The gospel contains a record of what Jesus *did* and *taught*,[26] and Paul teaches his hearers clearly

---

[23] Wilckens, *KDB* 1, p. 87.

[24] Cf. R. Schnackenburg in *BZ* 7 (1963), pp. 10–12.

[25] On the relationship between the deeds (miracles) and words of Jesus in the fourth gospel see W. Thüsing, *Die Erhöhung und Verherrlichung Jesu im Johannes-evangelium* (1960), pp. 58f., 152f., 154f., 181f.; H. Schlier, "Meditationen über den johanneischen Begriff der Wahrheit" in *Martin Heidegger zum siebzigsten Geburtstag* (1959), p. 189 on Jn 17:17: "The word that sets the disciples in the truth and makes them true is the (abiding) word of God that comes from the mouth of Jesus and is in Jesus' words and the signs performed by him." R. Formesyn, "Le sèmeion johannique et le sèmeion hellénistique", *ETL* 38 (1962), pp. 890f.

[26] Cf. "In the first book, O Theophilus, I have dealt with all that Jesus began to do and teach . . ." (Acts 1:1).

and unequivocally that it is by his words that God 'calls' men to newness of life,[27] and by his faithfulness to his words that he preserves this life for his own.[28]

For all the variations in the particular attitudes and approaches contained in the New Testament, therefore, a single general view prevails throughout it. It is that whereas God speaks in the Old Testament and provides testimony of Jesus in it, Jesus himself has revealed God to men not only by his actions and miracles but also by the words with which he has taught them. Thus the opening words of the Epistle to the Hebrews provide an accurate summary of the biblical doctrine of divine revelation when they define revelation as a 'speaking to' man on God's part at various times and in various ways: 'At various times and in various ways God spoke of old to our fathers by the prophets; but in these last days he has spoken to us by (the) Son . . .' (1:1 f.).[29]

In view of the sound arguments for rejecting the identification of revelation with history, which have been drawn from the

[27] On the 'call' of God in Paul cf. H. Schlier, *Der Brief an die Epheser* (2nd ed., 1958), pp. 82 ff. and E. Neuhäusler, "Ruf Gottes und Stand der Christen", *BZ* 3 (1959), p. 51; O. Kuss, *Der Römerbrief* (1957 ff.), p. 286, emphasizes that it is only by a misconception that history can be identified with divine revelation in Paul. According to Paul the believer regards history with the eyes of one who has been instructed by divine revelation.

[28] D. Wiederkehr, *Die Theologie der Berufung in den Paulusbriefen* (1963), p. 249: "That the eschatological event initiated by the call will not stop short, but will be carried through to its consummation is something that is guaranteed by the effective and active *faithfulness* of God, a quality essentially inherent in his grace and love (1 Cor 1:9; 1 Thess 5:24). The faith and trust of the one who is called can find support in the faithfulness of God in fulfilling his promises (Rom 4:17). This faithfulness of God guarantees the continuity of his action, by which he comes to the help of the one called, working for what is best for him and for his salvation in all things, even in adversities (Rom 8:28). God never goes back upon the graces and callings which he has once bestowed; they remain irrevocably in force (Rom 11:29)." For the significance of the 'faithfulness' of God for 'vocation' see *ibid.,* pp. 57, 116, 170, 185, 267.

[29] Cf. O. Michel, *Der Brief an die Hebräer* (11th ed., 1960), pp. 34 ff.; R. Schnackenburg in *BZ* 7 (1963), pp. 3–7.

Old and New Testaments, the attempt of W. Pannenberg, R. Rendtorff and U. Wilckens must be regarded as one-sided. As the texts of the Old and New Testaments tell us, we should not be led into minimizing the role attributed to the words spoken by God in Scripture by over-emphasizing the meaning latent in his divine actions and the manifestations of his power.

The formula 'revelation as history', and the attempts which have been made to establish its credentials from the Bible, remind us of a danger of which Plato warns us, that namely of becoming enemies of the word.[30] While on the one hand to find nothing but the 'address' of God in the Bible amounts to a misconception of what the Bible itself says (a fact which is impressively brought out precisely in the essays collected in *KDB* 1), it is no less inadmissible on the other to minimize the function of the word in the Bible and in human history. Pannenberg may be allowed to be right when he says that it is inadmissible to take all the statements of the modern 'personalist' theology of the word as gospel,[31] but when he rejects the 'personalist concept of the word' and "associates it with a Gnostic understanding of the word"[32] he goes too far and, moreover, contradicts the evidence of the Bible itself.

[30] Plato *Phaedo,* 89 C–D; F. Ebner, *Schriften* I (1963), p. 77 has put this passage amongst others at the beginning of his book "Das Wort und die geistigen Realitäten". On the attitude which Pannenberg adopts towards Ebner cf. *KDB* 1, p. 14.

[31] H. Gollwitzer, *Die Existenz Gottes im Bekenntnis des Glaubens* (1963), p. 116, regards Pannenberg's theories as a "counter-blow against a kerygmatism that has sacrified the 'facts' to the word to such an extent that they have sunk into the oblivion of past history. As a result the indispensable contribution which they make to the Bible, and the fact that they provide the basis for all that is contained in it is no longer expressed, in default of suitable categories in which to express it. So much attention is devoted to the word that the importance of the real fact is forgotten, and there is a danger in this of losing sight of the truly historical character of revelation, and of reducing the content of faith to a set of universal truths."

[32] Cf. especially *KDB* 1, p. 14.

What receives far too cursory a treatment in the theory of 'revelation as history' (apart from the fact that it cannot be reconciled with what the writings of the Bible actually say) is the significance of the word for history, and the central place which it occupies in human life.

It is language that first makes it possible to say 'we'[33] (and not merely 'thou'), and thereby makes possible also human community and human history.[34] Without the word that communicates, commands and promises men can neither 'make' history nor 'experience' it.[35] The history of Israel is no exception to this. Even supposing that a group of men could be found who had a history devoid of words, this would no longer have any relevance, at any rate for that stage in cultural development about which the Bible tells us.

If the Bible cannot be adduced to establish the thesis that 'the self-revelation of God has ... been achieved indirectly through God's deeds in history'[36] the question of biblical revelation

[33] In underestimating the role of the word in this manner it is once more apparent that adherents of the school of thought which Pannenberg represents have become enmeshed in the metaphysics of Descartes (cf. p. 41). On the problem of the 'word' in this sense, and on the connected problem of the 'dialogue' in the philosophy of Descartes, Hegel and Nietzsche, cf. F. Wiplinger, "Dialogischer Logos: Gedanken zur Struktur des Gegenüber", *Philosophisches Jahrbuch* 70 (1962/63), pp. 177 ff., though his explanations have a somewhat forced effect.

[34] Cf. G. Müller, "Zum Problem der Sprache, Erwägungen im Anschluß an das Sprachdenken Eugen Rosenstock-Huessys", *KD* 2 (1956), p. 149. In this connection reference should also be made to the work of J. G. Hamann, cf. W. Leibrecht, "Philologia Crucis. Johann Georg Hamanns Gedanken über die Sprache Gottes", *KD* 1 (1955), pp. 226–42. In view of the fact that the human mode of existence is of its essence characterized by the use of speech how far does the spoken word hold a pre-eminent place among all the media of revelation which can be conceived of? This question is investigated by H. Noack, *Sprache und Offenbarung. Zur Grenzbestimmung von Sprachphilosophie und Sprachtheologie* (1960).

[35] On the essential connection between word and history see further H. U. v. Balthasar, *Das Ganze im Fragment* (1963), pp. 245 ff.

[36] *KDB* 1, p. 91.

and the truth it contains must be posed anew and must be answered on a fresh basis. Our investigations so far have led to the conclusion that the bible speaks *both* of God's deeds in history *and* of his 'word', and that he reveals himself in both together. It therefore remains to investigate, in the pages which follow, what degree of importance the bible attributes to the word of God as compared with his deeds in history, and what deductions may be drawn from this for the question of the truth of Scripture. In other words we are putting the question of the significance of the 'covenant' for the truth of the Bible, as will be shown in the chapter which follows.

Vatican II. With its strong emphasis on the fact that word and deed belong together, the Constitution *Dei Verbum* clearly speaks the language of the Bible, and thereby, as is to be shown later, presupposes the biblical concept of truth. In particular mention must be made of the following passages: ch. I, art. 2: "This plan of revelation is realized by deeds and words having an inner unity: the deeds wrought by God in the history of salvation manifest and confirm the teaching and realities signified by the words, while the words proclaim the deeds and clarify the mystery contained in them. By this revelation, then, the deepest truth about God and the salvation of man is made clear to us in Christ, who is the Mediator and at the same time the fulness of all revelation." Ch. I, art. 4: ". . . through his words and deeds"; ch. II, art. 17: "This gospel had been promised in former times through the prophets, and Christ himself fulfilled it and promulgated it with his own lips . . ."; ch. V, art. 17: "Christ established the kingdom of God on earth, manifested his Father and himself by deeds and words . . ."; ch. V, art. 19: ". . . what Jesus the Son of God . . . really did and taught . . . the apostles handed on . . . what he had said and done . . ."

CHAPTER FOUR

COVENANT WITH ISRAEL AND REVELATION

A first conclusion to which the considerations so far put forward have led is that it is impossible to arrive at an acceptable definition of revelation merely by assembling those references to it in the Bible which are supposed to be particularly pregnant with meaning. If we rely on florilegia of this kind we shall stick fast at the preliminary stages of our investigation, for they fail to take cognizance of the whole context and milieu within which revelation was imparted to Israel. On the other hand, while 'revelation as history' turns out to be a blind alley, this should not drive us into a headlong retreat in the opposite direction, that is to placing a false and misconceived emphasis on the 'word' contained in Scripture. Nor can there be any question of finding a new and better method of assembling and correlating those passages which speak of God revealing himself either by manifesting his power or by his word. What we have to do, rather, is this: we must lay bare the historical reasons enabling us to understand why the references to God's revelation in Scripture should take the form of statements of what God said or what God did. Viewed from this standpoint the absolutely fundamental event was, I suggest, the institution of the covenant, the *berît*[1] between Yahweh and Israel.

[1] *Berît* signifies 'bond' or 'pact', cf. O. Loretz in *VT* 16 (1966), pp. 239–41. The division recently suggested once more by K.-M. Deller, *Bib* 47 (1966), hardly carries conviction.

With regard to the interpretations of the covenant of Sinai a turning-point has emerged in Old Testament exegesis.[2] In his *Prolegomena* J. Wellhausen writes as follows: "Theocracy was not in existence from the time of Moses onwards even in that form which later became so much beloved, the covenant. From the outset the relationship between Yahweh and Israel was a natural one. There was then no intervening gulf, no 'between' to separate him from his people, such as might have been the subject of subsequent reflexion and adaptation. It was not until ... prophets such as Elijah and Amos .. had made of the Godhead something exalted far above the people that the natural bond between the two was severed and replaced by a relationship that depended for its preservation on the observance of certain conditions and, in fact, of moral conditions ... In actual fact it was in this way that the idea of the covenant (i.e. pact) emerged; while the earlier ideas from which it derived were evident, the covenant itself was something wholly new ... Ever since the occasion on which, by a solemn and momentous act, Josiah

---

[2] On the question of the 'covenant' cf. the following: R. Kraetzschmar, *Die Bundesvorstellung im Alten Testament in ihrer geschichtlichen Entwicklung* (1896); P. Karge, *Die Geschichte des Bundesgedankens im Alten Testament* (1910); J. Begrich, "Berit, Ein Beitrag zur Erfassung einer alttestamentlichen Denkform", *ZAW* 60 (1944), pp. 1–11; M. Noth, "Das alttestamentliche Bundesschließen im Lichte eines Mari-Textes", *Gesammelte Studien zum Alten Testament* (1957), pp. 142–54; J. Muilenburg, "The Form and Structure of the Covenantal Formulations", *VT* 9 (1959), pp. 347–65; G. E. Mendenhall, *Law and Covenant in Israel and the Ancient Near East* (1955); K. Baltzer, *Das Bundesformular* (1960); M. Weise, *Kultzeiten und kultischer Bundesschluß in der 'Ordensregel' vom Toten Meer* (1961); F. C. Fensham, "The Possibility of the Presence of Casuistic Legal Material at the Making of the Covenant at Sinai", *PEQ* 33 (1961), pp. 143–6; F. Auer, "Das Alte Testament in der Sicht des Bundesgedankens" in *Lex tua Veritas — Festschrift H. Junker* (1961), pp. 1–16; W. L. Moran, "Moses und der Bundesschluß Sinai", *Stimmen der Zeit* 170/87 (1961–62), pp. 120–33; F. C. Fensham, "Malediction and Benediction in Ancient Near Eastern Vassal-Treaties and the Old Testament", *ZAW* 74 (1962), pp. 1–9; H. Gross, "Der Sinai-Bund als Lebensform des auserwählten Volkes im Alten Testament" in *Ekklesia — Festschrift M. Wehr* (1962), pp. 1–15; N. Lohfink,

introduced this law (of Deuteronomy), the idea of the making of a covenant between Yahweh and Israel seems to have been thrust into the centre of her religious thought . . .."[3] These considerations of Wellhausen are based upon the hypothesis that the institution of the covenant, however important its results may have been, took place not at the beginning of the history of Israel but at a late point in its development.

In the period after Wellhausen attempts were made to confirm this theory of his by means of a comprehensive investigation. Notable among these attempts is that of R. Kraetzschmar. According to this author's own explicit assertion he proceeds simply upon the well-founded assumption that as an Israelite institution the covenant was transferred to the sphere of religion from that of the profane. This is, after all, "the line of development followed by all religious concepts".[4] In his blind confidence in the hypothesis of the 'sources' Kraetzschmar regards it as an established fact that "in none of the eighth-century prophets . . . can any indication be found to support the position that the religious relationship

"der Bundesschluß im Land Moab", *BZ* 6 (1962), pp. 32–56; F. C. Fensham, "Clauses of Protection in Hittite Vassal-Treaties and the Old Testament", *VT* 13 (1963), pp. 133–43; J. Coppens, "La nouvelle alliance en Jer 31:31–34", *CBQ* 25 (1963), pp. 12–21; M. Delcor, "Das Bundesfest in Qumran und das Pfingstfest", *Bibel und Leben* 4 (1963), pp. 188–209; A. Jaubert, *La Notion de l'Alliance dans le Judaïsme aux abords de l'ère chrétienne* (1963); M. G. Kline, *Treaty of the Great King. The Covenant Structure of Deuteronomy* (1963); N. Lohfink, *Das Hauptgebot. Eine Untersuchung literarischer Einleitungsfragen zu Dtn 5–11* (1963), pp. 108 ff.; id., "Die Bundesurkunde des Königs Josias (Eine Frage an die Deuteronomiumsforschung)", *Bib* 44 (1963), pp. 261–88; D. J. McCarthy, *Treaty and Covenant* (1963); id., "Three Covenants in Genesis", *CBQ* 26 (1964), pp. 179–89; R. Smend, *Die Bundesformel* (1963); A. Deissler, "Die wesentliche Bundesweisung in der mosaischen und frühprophetischen Gottesbotschaft", *Gott in Welt — Festgabe für K. Rahner,* vol. I (1964), pp. 445–62; R. Frankena, "The Vassal-Treaties of Essarhadon and the Dating of Deuteronomy", *OTS* 14 (1965), pp. 122–54.

[3] J. Wellhausen, *Prolegomena zur Geschichte Israels* (5th ed., 1899), pp. 423 f.

[4] R. Kraetzschmar, *Die Bundesvorstellung im Alten Testament in ihrer geschichtlichen Entwicklung,* p. 6.

between Yahweh and Israel was based upon a *berît* which had been instituted between them".[5] According to Kraetzschmar, therefore, the only evidence for the existence of the covenant idea is late, and the covenant itself would not have been instituted before the 7th century. The conclusions he comes to concerning the covenant are vitiated by this view: "Regarded purely from the religious point of view it (the idea of the covenant) represents, however, a retrograde step from the elevated knowledge of God which appears in the prophets."[6] Thus the following estimate is given of the value of the covenant idea: "It represents a compromise between the prophetic ideal on the one hand, and the powers of assimilation of the broader masses of the people on the other."[7]

Fourteen years after Kraetzschmar's book had appeared P. Karge published his comprehensive study (439 pages) on the covenant.[8] By this time some texts of ancient Near Eastern literature were already available, and Karge sought by using these to take sources and not hypotheses as the starting-point for his investigation of the problem of the covenant. In summarizing his conclusions he could say of his work: "Moreover it has been found possible to show that according to our current knowledge, the cultural and religious situation in the Near East, and of the Israelite people at the time of their entry into Canaan, was such that a religion of the nature of the covenant religion was indeed possible."[9]

In accordance with the maxim *'Pro captu lectoris habent sua fata libelli'* (Terentius Maurus 258) this work, in spite of its author's careful use of the ancient Near Eastern material available at that time, must have been considered too conservative at the time when it appeared, and therefore as unworthy of notice. The 439 pages written by Karge had no influence on exegetical trends. The time was not yet ripe for a book of this sort. The book was *non avenu,* did not find acceptance.

---

[5] *Ibid.,* p. 122. [6] *Ibid.,* p. 146. [7] *Ibid.*
[8] P. Karge, *Die Geschichte des Bundesgedankens im AT.* [9] *Ibid.*

Another article on the covenant which has attracted much attention is that of J. Begrich. Here too no fundamental departure from previously held theories can be discerned.[10] Thus Begrich too contends that in the early period there was no connection between the covenant itself and the obligations which it was subsequently held to entail for the human partners to it, ". . . in other words a connection between *berît* and law. From this a vital conclusion follows: the circumstances leading up to the issuing of laws cannot be explained upon the basis of the *berît* idea."[11] According to Begrich it was 'only under the potent influence of Canaanite ideas of justice'[12] that this idea of legal obligation was introduced into the concept of covenant.

In the meantime, however, the ground had already been cleared for a radical departure from previously held theories. In his study of the Decalogue S. Mowinckel[13] had already pointed out the cultic elements in the description of the theophany at Sinai (Ex 19), and he had shown that the covenant was not merely a late idea in Wellhausen's sense. Then M. Noth worked out what the institution must have been which lay behind the annual renewal of the covenant, already connected by Mowinckel with a festival of the New Year. According to Noth this would have been a confederation of the twelve tribes going back to the premonarchist period of Israel's history.[14] Next in 1934 A. Alt showed that there were reasons for believing that the so-called 'apodictic law' in the decalogue was extremely ancient.[15]

The study of G. E. Mendenhall, *Law and Covenant in Israel*

---

[10] J. Begrich, "Berit. Ein Beitrag zur Erfassung einer alttestamentlichen Denkform", *ZAW* 60 (1944), pp. 1–11.

[11] *Ibid.*, p. 7.

[12] *Ibid.*, p. 4.

[13] S. Mowinckel, *Le Décalogue* (1927).

[14] M. Noth, *Das System der zwölf Stämme Israels* (1930).

[15] A. Alt, "Die Ursprünge des israelitischen Rechts", *Kleine Schriften,* I (1953), pp. 278–332.

and the Ancient Near East[16] marks a decisive step forward in the discussion of the problem of the covenant. Whereas Begrich still makes the binding force of the law separate from the covenant, Mendenhall combines them: "The major question is whether or not that federation of tribes had a precursor in the nomadic period before the entry into Canaan. The present writer believes that the federation of tribes can be understood and explained only on the assumption that it is a conscious continuation and re-adaptation of an earlier tradition which goes back to the time of Moses. The covenant at Sinai was the formal means by which the semi-nomadic clans, recently emerged from state slavery in Egypt, were bound together in a religious and political community. The text of that covenant is the Decalogue."[17]

But how can it be explained that the element of law is so prominent in the covenant of Sinai? Mendenhall sees a way towards understanding what took place at Sinai in the fact "that there is a type of covenant preserved in ancient Oriental sources which may be of use in arriving at some tentative conclusions concerning all of the problems mentioned above. This is the suzerainty treaty by which a great king bound his vassals to faithfulness and obedience to himself."[18]

K. Baltzer has come to similar conclusions[19] independently of Mendenhall. The works mentioned above have shown that in the making of the covenant between Yahweh and Israel a treaty formula was employed that must have been in general and widespread use at the time,[20] since otherwise there would be no

---

[16] G. E. Mendenhall, *Law and Covenant in Israel and the Ancient Near East*. This work was first published in *BA* 17 (1954), pp. 24–46, 49–76.

[17] *Ibid.*, pp. 7–8.   [18] *Ibid.*, p. 29.   [19] *BF,* p. 17, n. 6.

[20] Cf. Mendenhall, *Law and Covenant,* pp. 30 f. On the question of how Israel could have come to know of this treaty form W. L. Moran observes in his article, "Moses und der Bundesschluß am Sinai", p. 129: "It might be objected, how could Moses or the Israelites be familiar with a form which has come down to us only in Anatolian, North Syrian and North Mesopotamian records? Our answer to this is that we have indirect, but nonetheless note-

way of explaining why Israel entered into this particular kind of union with her God. The form of revelation described in the Bible and peculiar to it is one in which God reveals himself in word and deed. How far this is conditioned by the special form of covenant-making which we have been considering must now be examined in still closer detail.

As K. Baltzer has convincingly shown, similarities[21] do exist between the political treaties of the Hittites (in the present state of the sources these offer the best examples available[22]) and the covenant as formulated in the Old Testament. This plan of the Hittite treaties is a follows:[23]

1. Preamble
2. Previous History
3. Declaration of Principle concerning the future relationship between the parties
4. Particular prescriptions
5. Calling of the gods to witness
6. Curse and blessing.[24]

worthy evidence in 14th century texts for the existence of this form in the area of the Phoenician coast, Palestine and Egypt. These are included among the Amarna Letters, that is in the correspondence of the Pharaohs with the independent empires of Babylon, Assyria, Mitanni and Hatti, and also with their own vassal kingdoms in Syria, Phoenicia and Palestine. We have no reason to believe that the knowledge of this form would have been lost by the following century."

[21] In his criticism, *Bib* 43 (1962), pp. 100–106, W. L. Moran agrees with this point and carries it further. For a criticism of earlier publications on the relationship between the Hittite treaties and the Old Testament covenant formular cf. Fr. Nötscher, "Bundesformular und 'Amtsschimmel'", *BZ* 9 (1965), pp. 181–214.

[22] Cf. W. L. Moran, "Moses und der Bundesschluß am Sinai", p. 123.

[23] *BF*, pp. 20 ff. In his work, *Treaty and Covenant*, pp. 15–106, which goes further than that of Baltzer, D. J. McCarthy distinguishes between the Hittite and the Assyrian-Syrian traditions. Since in this context we are concerned only with sketching in the historical background to covenant making in the Old Testament, it is enough to adduce one tradition only.

[24] D. J. McCarthy, *Treaty and Covenant,* pp. 25 and 41, distinguishes between

In the 'preamble' the name of the overlord who is making the treaty is given, and in the 'previous history' attached to this a description is given of the relationship between the empire of the overlord on the one hand and the land and person of the vassal on the other. This 'previous history' can extend over as many as five generations, and in this section the chief emphasis is laid upon the favours (bestowal of land etc.) performed by the overlord, which are described in appropriate terms. The section of the treaty that comprises the 'declaration of principle concerning the future relationship of the parties' is especially prominent in treaties which are formulated after the Hittite pattern. This part of the treaty is the outcome of the description of the previous favours bestowed by the overlord; at the same time it leads on to the 'particular prescriptions' which follow. In the 'declaration of principle' only universal imperatives are found, and, reduced to basic terms, what they demand is the loyalty of the other party to the treaty. The particular stipulations of the treaty which follow this are usually expressed in conditional form according to the following pattern: "If such-and-such an eventuality should ensue, you shall behave in such-and-such a manner." This part of the treaty is taken up with the various legal rights and obligations, and the problems which arise in connection with them. In the treaties the gods are then summoned as 'witnesses'. The gods are not merely witnesses, however, who verify the fact that a treaty has been concluded. They are at the same time guarantors that the conditions of the treaty will be implemented. They will persecute those who break the oath

Hittite parity treaties and Hittite vassal treaties. In the former the order is: 1) Mutual titulature; 2) History of past relations; 3) Affirmation of brotherhood; 4) Stipulations; 5) List of divine witnesses; 6) Curses and blessings; 7) [Addendum concerning fugitives]. In the vassal treaties the form is: 1) Titulature; 2) History; 3) Stipulations; 4) List of divine witnesses; 5) Curses and Blessings. How far the accounts given up till now will have to be corrected by the discovery of fresh texts is not yet finally apparent. It would not be possible at the present stage to arrive at any ultimate picture.

with their 'curse' and, conversely, will reward those who are loyal to the treaty.

The setting down of the treaty in writing is of great importance. This emerges from the very fact that the phrase "to write the tablet of the treaty" is synonymous with "to guarantee the treaty relationship". The "expunging" of the tablet signifies the end of the treaty. The original or a duplicate is laid up "at the feet" of the chief deities of the lands participating in it. In this way knowledge of the treaty is to be kept alive. The prescription that the text of the treaty is to be read in the presence of the vassal at regular intervals has the same end in view.

The pattern of the Hittite vassal treaty described here is also apparent either wholly or in part in numerous passages of the Old Testament. In his study[25] Baltzer treats of the form of the covenant of Shechem (Josh 24), that contained in the 'Sinai' pericope (Ex 19:3–8; 24:3–4a, 7), and the covenant formulation in Deuteronomy (Deut 1–4; 28:69 — 30:20). In conclusion Baltzer discusses the "covenant form used in the renewal of the covenant" (Ex 34; Neh 9–19; Ezra 9–10; Dan 9:4b–19; 1 QS I 18–II 18), the circumstances leading to a renewal of the covenant (2 Chron 29:5–11; 2 Chron 14:8–15:15; 2 Kings 22–23; Jer 44:8–22; 2 Kings 18–19; Jer 21:1–7; Josh 7–8; 1 Kings 8), the occasion on which the covenant was renewed, the form of covenant employed when the covenant was confirmed (Josh 23; 1 Sam 12; Deut 31 — Josh 1; 1 Chron 22–29; 2 Kings 11), how the covenant form is related to 'testament', and the formal reading of the covenant text.

Of all the above mentioned passages which have a bearing upon the form of the covenant used, it may be taken that the most important is the account of the covenant at Sinai. Selecting this, then, for special examination, we arrive at the following picture:[26]

---

[25] *BF,* pp. 29 ff.
[26] Cf. M. Noth, *Das zweite Buch Mose (Exodus)* (1959), pp. 121 ff.; *BF,* pp. 37 ff.; W. L. Moran, "Moses und der Bundesschluß am Sinai", pp. 126 ff. As D. J.

First an account is given of the preparation for the covenant. In Yahweh's name Moses addresses the Israelites in the following terms: "Thus shall you say to the house of Jacob and tell the people of Israel: You have seen what I did to the Egyptians, and how I bore you on eagle's wings and brought you to myself. Now therefore if you will obey my voice and keep my covenant, you shall be my own possession among all peoples, for all the earth is mine. And you shall be to me a kingdom of priests and a holy nation. These are the words which you shall speak to the children of Israel" (Ex 19 : 3–6).

Taking this offer of a covenant as our starting-point, we can plainly discern the logical sequence of the ensuing elements: history, covenant conditions, blessings. After three days spent in preparation Israel goes out to meet her God (Ex 19 : 10–17). This time Yahweh addresses the people directly, and Moses does not act as his intermediary: "I am Yahweh, your God, who brought you out of the land of Egypt, out of the house of bondage. You shall have no other gods before me . . . You shall not make yourself a graven image . . ." (Ex 20 : 2 ff.). After Yahweh has presented himself by uttering his name, he recalls the history which has led up to this point; then follows (in the commandments Ex 20 : 3–17) the 'declaration of principle'.

In the concluding ceremonies (Ex 24) Moses repeats Yahweh's words and the people declare their assent to them anew. Moses then writes down the text of the covenant in "the book of the covenant". Twelve stone pillars are set up. These, like the ones mentioned in Josh 24, are to serve as witnesses to the twelve tribes[27] who have entered into the treaty. The covenant is then

McCarthy, *Treaty and Covenant,* pp. 152–67, shows, the standpoint from which the events of the making of the covenant at Sinai are represented in the accounts is one in which all the emphasis is laid upon the apparition of God. In the Old Testament it is not a direct copy of the pact that is handed down, but narratives and sermons concerning pacts (cf. E. Gerstenberger, *JBL* 83 [1964], p. 199).

[27] Steles inscribed with the text of a treaty were described as "houses of the

sealed by the sprinkling of the altar (which represents Yahweh) and the people with blood (Ex 24:6–8).[28] The priests and the seventy elders of the people then ascend the mountain of God, and here, in the course of a ceremonial meal which is symbolic of the new covenant between Israel and her God, they "behold Yahweh".

In this presentation of the events no account is given of the depositing of the written document in the sanctuary or in the ark. The account of the setting up of the ark of the covenant, the place where the text of the treaty was laid up for safe keeping,[29] was only added later.

Shortly after the covenant was made Israel fell into an act of infidelity by worshipping the golden calf. In his anger at this Moses smashed the tablets. Their destruction signified that the covenant was abrogated. If Israel was to continue to be Yahweh's people, the covenant would have to be renewed, and the document which had been destroyed would have to be replaced by a new one. Hence the repetition of the making of the covenant (Ex 34:1–35).

This covenant which was made under Moses[30] was the first covenant between Yahweh and Israel. From this point onwards the history of God's relationship with his people developed along lines determined by the covenant. The factor which decided

gods". They were considered as the dwelling-places of those gods whose names were recorded as guarantees of the treaty; cf. H. Donner, "Zu Genesis 28:22", *ZAW* 74 (1962), pp. 68–70.

[28] On the remote connection between this rite and that of dividing a beast into two halves at the making of a pact (Gen 15), and on the significance of the blood cf. J. Henninger, "Was bedeutet die rituelle Teilung eines Tieres in zwei Hälften?", *Bib* 34 (1953), p. 351; J. E. Steinmüller, "Sacrificial Blood in the Bible", *Bib* 40 (1959), pp. 556–67.

[29] On the different views concerning the origin of the ark tradition cf. M. Noth, *Das zweite Buch Mose,* pp. 164 ff.; W. L. Moran, "Moses und der Bundesschluß am Sinai", p. 127.

[30] On the various modern theories concerning the personality of Moses cf. R. Smend, *Das Mosebild von Heinrich Ewald bis Martin Noth* (1959).

what direction the ensuing history was to take was the fidelity or infidelity of the people to the covenant (cf. the Old Testament passages on the covenant adduced above). In this respect Israel stands out as unique; among all the peoples surrounding her no comparable instance can be found, for the idea of a treaty between a people and its own God is unknown apart from Israel.[31]

K. Baltzer is therefore right in stating that "It will always remain matter for astonishment that the relationship between Israel and her God as experienced and known by her is expressed in so sober a form. This form is connected with her history, and at the same time with her law. In this respect Israel's religion is certainly different from that which passed for 'religion' in the world about her, for here the gods are made known in the first instance in the regular and periodic processes of nature, and in cult myths. Israel, on the contrary, recognizes that Yahweh has revealed himself in history. Israel knows that Yahweh is a God of justice and not one of arbitrary caprice".[32]

The institution of the covenant is an event which is central to the history of Israel. From this event, and from the special structure of the covenant itself, it can be deduced that the following factors play a decisive part in determining the character of divine revelation and its truth:

1. The deeds of God in history are intrinsically connected with, and ordered to the covenant, and thereby to the word of God. Thus for instance the exodus from Egypt cannot be regarded in isolation from other deeds of salvation performed by God.[33] The tradition concerning the exodus is intrinsically connected with the tradition of the making of the covenant and forms a historical prologue to it.[34] More than any other event

---

[31] Cf. A. Falkenstein in *BF,* p. 97, n. 3.

[32] *Ibid.,* p. 97 f.

[33] Thus for instance W. Pannenberg, *KDB* 1, 91: ". . . Exodus from Egypt . . . with that event, therefore, which, as far as ancient Israel was concerned, was the basic deed of salvation performed by Yahweh."

[34] On the question of how the 'Sinai' and 'Exodus' traditions are related to

the exodus from Egypt provides the basis for God's claim to Israel's service,[35] and directly precedes the event of Sinai.[36] Even in the period following upon this the actions of God are connected with the covenant. In them Yahweh manifests his fidelity to the covenant and through the medium of his actions he punishes his people when they break the covenant. In the history during and after the exile history itself recedes into the background, and attention is turned more and more to the sinfulness of the people (Neh 9; Ps 106). These factors now exercise an influence upon the way in which the covenant is understood. The law acquires a central importance and an absolute and independent status.[37] That the covenant idea is not thereby obscured, however, is shown by the covenant renewal ceremonies held every year.[38]

2. Since the manifestations of Yahweh's power prepare the way for the acceptance of the covenant, it follows that they are ordered to the 'word'. For the making of the covenant presupposes that he who offers the treaty makes his will known in specific words. In the case under consideration these are the laws of the covenant[39] and the threats or promises for the future contained

one another cf. W. L. Moran, "Moses und der Bundesschluß am Sinai", pp. 128 ff.

[35] On the significance of the 'Exodus' tradition see, amongst other works, H. Lubsczyk, *Der Auszug Israels aus Ägypten. Seine theologische Bedeutung in prophetischer und priesterlicher Überlieferung* (1963). On the commemoration of the exodus and passover in the Old and New Testaments cf. N. Füglister, *Die Heilsbedeutung des Pascha* (1963), esp. pp. 233 ff., "Pasch and Covenant".

[36] W. Beyerlin (*Herkunft und Geschichte der ältesten Sinaitraditionen* [1961], p. 190) remarks on the relationship between the two traditions: "In conclusion, with regard to the relationship between it (the 'Sinai' tradition) and the 'Exodus' tradition, it must be maintained that both traditions were connected with each other right from the beginning of the covenant with Yahweh. The form of covenant already attested in the Hittite treaties of the 14th and 13th centuries is found underlying the decalogue too, the fundamental law of the Sinai covenant (II 15). This form includes a historical prologue which is a reminder of the favours previously bestowed by the institutor of the covenant."

[37] *BF*, pp. 98 f. [38] *BF*, pp. 68–70. [39] On the question of the laws cf. p. 17.

in the blessings and cursings. The people are exhorted to remain faithful to the words of the covenant. If they fall away, then the word of the curse will take effect. The will of the overlord, which is expressed in the word of the pact, is central to the covenant institution, and it follows from this as an assured conclusion that God also reveals himself through the word. By announcing his will God permits himself to be known.

3. In the institution of the covenant God reveals himself by word and deed as the unique God who does not tolerate any other gods besides himself (Ex 20:2).[40] At the exodus, already in the stages preparatory to the covenant the Lord of the covenant has shown himself to be one who has power over the gods of Egypt, and in the pact he requires of Israel that she shall serve him alone as her king.[41]

4. The covenant institution was decisive for the life of Israel, and determined the course of subsequent history, and thereby that of revelation too. In this way the form of the covenant had an influence, for example, on the prophetic literature. The prophets summon the people to a trial and arraign them for breach of the covenant.[42] Heaven and earth are summoned as

[40] In his article, "Sinn und Ursprung der priesterlichen Geschichtserzählung", *ZTK* 49 (1952), pp. 121–43, K. Elliger emphasizes that for the priestly conception of history the revelation of God's power has the force of a demonstration of his fidelity to the covenant (*ibid.*, pp. 138f., 141ff.).

[41] W. L. Moran ("Moses und der Bundesschluß", pp. 130f.) rightly emphasizes that the kingship of Yahweh already finds expression in the formulation of the covenant, for Yahweh is sovereign in relation to Israel just as the Hittite king is in relation to his vassal.

[42] J. Harvey, "Le 'Rîb-Pattern', réquisitoire prophétique sur la rupture de l'alliance", *Bib* 43 (1962), pp. 172–96. On Micah 6:1–8 see especially W. Beyerlin, *Die Kulturtraditionen Israels in der Verkündigung des Propheten Micha* (1959), pp. 69ff.; A. Deissler, "Micha 6:1–8. Der Rechtsstreit Jahwes mit Israel und das rechte Bundesverhältnis", *TrTZ* 68 (1959), pp. 229–34; N. Lohfink, *Das Hauptgebot,* pp. 134f. On the problem of why the word 'covenant' was not used by the prophets see W. Eichrodt, *Theologie des Alten Testaments,* vol. I (5th ed., 1957), pp. 19f., E. T.: *Theology of the Old Testament,* vol. I (1961), trans. by G. J. Baker; H. Wildberger, *VTS 9* (1963), pp. 104ff.

witnesses (Is 1:2; Jer 2:12; cf. Deut 4:26; 30:19; 31:28; 32:1),[43] and the prophets fearlessly uphold the rights of the covenant God.[44]

5. The event of the covenant institution also had an effect upon Israelite history writing in that it led those who wrote it to view even the prior history of Israel in the light of this momentous occurrence. In this way the writers of Israel's history came to regard and to judge history in general in the light of this moment in history, so decisive as it was for them. In practice the result of this was that the early history of Israel was interpreted as covenant history.[45] Thus we find mention of a covenant

[43] W. L. Moran, "Some Remarks on the Song of Moses (Dt 32)", *Bib* 43 (1962), pp. 317–20.

[44] A. Deissler, "Die wesentliche Bundesweisung in der mosaischen und früh-prophetischen Gottesbotschaft", p. 446: "The point of reference, whether explicit or implicit, of all prophetic preaching is henceforward always the Mosaic charter of the covenant."

[45] In his article, "Erfahrung in der Geschichte und Geschichtswissenschaft" in W. Strolz, ed., *Experiment und Erfahrung in Wissenschaft und Kunst* (1963), p. 240, A. Mirgeler remarks à propos of this problem of history writing: "An epoch-making event always arouses an historical interest that works retrospectively; it creates an area of interest about itself. For it causes one to think of a certain period of time as the past that converges upon the event in question. Whether it leads up to it, or away from it, or both makes no difference. This is the basis for Droysen's rule of historical interpretation: 'This new occurrence provides a perspective from which events (specifically designated by the author) *appear* ... as preparing for and conditioning the occurrence itself. Thus the pragmatic narrative proceeds from what are conceived to be its 'origins' in the past, and from these leads on to the present. It is this inversion of the real order that makes it possible to detach history from the present as a temporal sequence to which dates can be assigned and about which judgments are made. But it does *not* make it possible to go further than this and, without regard to the origins of history, to 'hypostasize' the 'flow' of it into a series of wholly autonomous 'presents', each of which is pregnant with decisions for the future. Still less is it possible to extend the hypostasis so formed endlessly into the future or up to an absolute end of all history. Moreover, it is never possible to regard an event as *necessarily* following from the conditions of the past.'"

of God with Noah (Gen 9:8–17) and above all of the making of a covenant with Abraham (Gen 15:9–12, 17f.; 17:1–14).[46] The institution of the covenant at Sinai is retrospectively projected into the early history of the people, and in this way comes to be recognized as the most significant event in the history of Israel.

The fact that the past came to be viewed in the light of the covenant which God made with Israel was not the only effect of the covenant of Sinai. The monarchy too was brought into connection with it. Thus the founding of the Davidic dynasty — E. Kutsch rightly calls it "the dynasty of God's grace"[47] — is understood as the institution of a covenant.[48] A guarantee of the 'covenant type' (the covenant of the Levites)[49] is also provided for the priestly succession of the Levites from Aaron (Num 18:19; Jer 33:20ff.; Ecclus 45:24).

In spite of all vicissitudes the covenant pattern continued to be a vital force right down to New Testament and early Christian times.[50] Then in the New Testament the idea of the covenant once more acquires a fresh significance, for Jesus himself — and among those who come after him particularly Paul — speaks of a new and final covenant, one which makes the Sinai covenant

---

[46] For an individual treatment of these instances cf. W. Eichrodt, *Theologie des Alten Testaments,* vol. I, pp. 18ff., 23; W. Zimmerli, "Sinaibund und Abrahambund. Ein Beitrag zum Verständnis der Priesterschrift", *TZ* 16 (1960), pp. 268–80, see further on the covenant idea in the Priestly tradition N. Lohfink, "Die Wandlung des Bundesbegriffs im Buch Deuteronomium" in *Gott in Welt — Festgabe für K. Rahner,* vol. I (1964), p. 442, n. 53. This author regards Ex 6:7 and not, as is often assumed, Lev 26:45, as the crucial passage for showing that in addition to the covenants with Noah and Abraham P also knows of a covenant at Sinai.

[47] E. Kutsch, "Die Dynastie von Gottes Gnaden, Probleme der Nathan-weissagung in 2 Sam 7", *ZTK* 58 (1961), pp. 137ff.

[48] A. H. J. Gunneweg, "Sinaibund und Davidsbund", *VT* 10 (1960), pp. 338 to 41. V. Hamp, *LTK,* vol. II, col. 773.

[49] W. Eichrodt, *Theologie des Alten Testaments,* vol. I (5th ed., 1957), E. T.: *The Theology of the Old Testament* (1961).

[50] *BF,* pp. 103–79 (The covenant form in Jewish and early Christian texts).

obsolete,[51] and thereby replaces the blood of the animal victims offered under the terms of the old covenant with the Blood of the new and eternal covenant.[52]

On the question of the truth of the Bible, what conclusions can be drawn from the fact that in the history of God with his people, made up as it is of words and deeds, the covenant occupies a central place? In answering this question we must emphasize two points: 1. Sacred Scripture is to be understood as a book which speaks in manifold ways of the covenant of God with his people — the tradition of the Church speaks of the Old Testament and the New as the books of the old and new covenants. 2. The question is raised: 'Having regard to its theme, the covenant of God with men, what specific kind of truth does the Bible recognize? When is the covenant true or false?' Concurrent with, and immediately parallel to this problem, is another one: 'By what standard are we to measure the truth of the books of this covenant?' Yet a further problem awaits investigation in connection with the relationship between Scripture and revelation. This relationship is to be viewed in the light of the covenant, and the problem is 'To what extent does Scripture contain the word of God in true and undistorted form?'[53]

Vatican II. In *Dei Verbum,* in accordance with sacred Scripture,

---

[51] On the problem of the covenant in the New Testament cf. Behm, *TWNT,* vol. II, pp. 132–7. L. Goppelt, *RGG* 1 (1957), cols. 1516–18; J. Schmid, *LTK,* vol. II, cols. 776–8; N. Lohfink, "Die Wandlung des Bundesbegriffes im Buch Deuteronomium" in *Gott in Welt, Festgabe für K. Rahner,* vol. I (1964), p. 443.

[52] Mt 26:28; Mk 14:24; Lk 22:20; 1 Cor 11:25; R. Schmid, *Das Bundesopfer in Israel. Wesen, Ursprung und Bedeutung der alttestamentlichen Schelamim,* (1964), pp. 125 f. On the central importance of the covenant idea in the life of Jesus and for the foundation of the Church cf. A. Vögtle, "Der Einzelne und die Gemeinschaft in der Stufenfolge der Christusoffenbarung", *Sentire Ecclesiam. Festschrift H. Rahner* (1961), p. 90; U. Horst, *MTZ* 16 (1965), p. 189.

[53] L. Alonso-Schökel (*Bib* 46 [1965], p. 380) puts forward the objection that even in connection with the covenant institution one cannot validly speak of the fidelity of God without any restriction. His argument runs as follows:

the revelation of God is viewed in the context of the covenant. Ch. IV, art. 14: "First he entered into a covenant with Abraham (cf. Gen 15:18) and, through Moses, with the people of Israel (cf. Ex 24: 8). To this people which he had acquired for himself he so manifested himself through words and deeds as the one true and living God ... ." The account of this event is contained in the Old Testament as the word of God. Ch. IV, art. 14: "The plan of salvation foretold by the sacred authors, recounted and explained by them, is found as the true word of God in the books of the Old Testament ..." This account is brought to completion in the New Testament, so that both books of the covenant are inseparably connected with one another. Ch. IV, art. 16: "God the inspirer and author of both Testaments wisely arranged that the New Testament be hidden in the Old, and the Old be made manifest in the New. For though Christ established the new covenant in his Blood (cf. Lk 22:20; 1 Cor 11:25), still the books of the Old Testament with all their parts, caught up into the proclamation of the gospel, acquire and show forth their full meaning in the New Testament (cf. Mt 5:17; Lk 24:27; Rom 16:25–26; 2 Cor 3:14–16), and in turn shed light upon it and explain it."[54]

"While the covenant as a fact is basic to the existence of the people, the deeds of salvation narrated in the prologue to it do not yet constitute acts of covenant fidelity, and the words in which those deeds are narrated are claimed to be true in a factual sense. The covenant provides the *basis for* fidelity on God's part but is not itself presented as an act of fidelity. It might represent fidelity to the word bestowed upon Abraham. But the author draws no clear distinction between covenant and promise. On the contrary he attempts to include all under the general heading of 'covenant'." In offering this criticism Alonso-Schökel is beating an open door, for I was considering the covenant chiefly from the aspect of the relationship of word to deed, and when I emphasized that it was the central event in the history of Israel I was not denying the point raised by Alonso-Schökel.

[54] Further on this see ch. V, art. 17. Cf. A. Grillmeier, "Die Wahrheit der Heiligen Schrift und ihre Erschließung. Zum dritten Kapitel der dogmatischen Konstitution 'Dei Verbum' des Vaticanum II", *ThPh* 1 (1966), p. 179: "Scripture is a special expression of the covenant faithfulness and the will to save of God."

CHAPTER FIVE

BIBLE'S CLAIM TO TRUTH

It can be said without exaggeration that the doctrine of the inspiration of Scripture is one of the most disputed and most frequently misunderstood of all theological doctrines. The question to be investigated here, therefore, is whether we cannot find a way of seeing the Bible's claim to be true in its correct light by taking as our starting-point the special nature of divine revelation as proceeding from a God who is related to his people as their covenant Lord.

The manuals of dogmatic theology, in line with ecclesiastical tradition, present the inerrancy of Scripture as the result of inspiration: "The inerrancy of sacred Scripture follows from the fact of inspiration. Any error contained in it would have to be attributed to the divine author himself. *Providentissimus Deus, DS* 1951; *Decretum Lamentabili, DS* 2011, 2014; *Spiritus Paraclitus.*"[1] Although their formulation is somewhat different, Pohle-Gummersbach and Diekamp-Jüssen agree with M. Schmaus on this point. In Pohle-Gummersbach it is stated as follows: "The effect of inspiration is that all the statements in Scripture, whether religious or profane, are infallibly true in that sense which their author intended them to bear, and in that form in which they were recorded by him. Fidei proximum."[2] Diekamp-

---

[1] M. Schmaus, *Katholische Dogmatik,* vol. I (6th ed., 1960), p. 128, § 15.
[2] Pohle-Gummersbach, *Lehrbuch der Dogmatik,* vol. I (10th ed., 1952), p. 56.

Jüssen, however, lays down that "Sacred Scripture is free from error. Fidei proximum."[3]

In the course of history inerrancy has been variously interpreted. Augustine writes: "Those books of Scripture that are called canonical, and these alone, I have learnt to regard with such attention and reverence that I believe as something that is most sure that none of their authors has erred in the writing of them. If I come upon anything in Scripture which seems contrary to the truth I shall not hesitate to consider that it is no more than a faulty reading of the manuscript, or a failure of the translator to hit off what his text declared, or that I have not succeeded in understanding the passage" (*Epist.* 82).[4] Now the implication of this would be that biblical inerrancy is to be identified with the ideal of the perfection of a book. Augustine was not alone among the ancients in holding this. It is maintained by other writers of the Church as well, and, moreover, it was subsequently taken up by the theologians of the Middle Ages.[5]

A factor to be borne in mind in considering this championing of biblical inerrancy, extremely vigorous as it has often been, is that it represents a defensive reaction against those who have tended to see nothing but errors in Scripture, and have sought for this reason to bring Scripture as the book of revelation into discredit. It is apparent from the history of the Church viewed as a whole that from the moment when it was first raised, this question of inerrancy has never been settled altogether satisfactorily.

Amid the conflict of views which have been put forward over the years this much at least has emerged as a hard core of truth that the claim that accurate scientific knowledge is to be found in Scripture cannot be upheld. In the trial of Galileo, to take

---

[3] Diekamp-Jüssen, *Katholische Dogmatik nach den Grundsätzen des heiligen Thomas,* vol. I (13th ed., 1958), p. 40, § 11.

[4] Augustine, Ep. LXXXII, I, 3; *CSEL,* XXXIV, p. 354, lines 4–11.

[5] Cf. the passages adduced in *DBS* 4 (1949), cols. 525 ff. See also P. Zerafa, "The Limits of Biblical Inerrancy", *Angelicum* 39 (1962), pp. 92 f.

only one particularly well-known example, Scripture was still being invoked against the statements of natural science. Thus for instance it was believed that the passage in Ecclesiastes 1:4: "A generation goes and a generation comes but the earth remains for ever", must necessarily be interpreted as meaning that the earth stands still and does not move. Yet nowadays no-one would claim that this sort of truth is contained in Scripture. The fact remains, however, that up to the present no generally accepted formula has been worked out to express the fact that Scripture is not intended to inculcate the truths of natural science. Thus with reference to the statements in Scripture which have a bearing on natural science Diekamp-Jüssen writes: "The sacred authors often speak of the processes of nature as they appear to the senses (I, q. 70, a. 1, 3: *secutus est [ea] quae sensibiliter apparent*), or by means of images or in the popular idiom and mode of expression (*Providentissimus Deus, DS* 1947). Such modes of expression may well run counter to the scientific knowledge of today. They are none the less true for that, for the truth which they are intended to convey is not that of science but that of sensible appearance. The authors were compelled to write in this manner so as to be understood by all. In the purposes of God sacred Scripture is meant to instruct us men in religion, and to help us to obtain eternal salvation. Now an exact knowledge of the nature of visible objects has no salvific value. 'Spiritus Dei qui per ipsos (scriptores sacros) loquebatur, noluit ista docere homines nulli saluti profutura' (Augustine, *De Genesi ad Litteram,* II, 9, 20).[6]

What is being asserted here, then, is that statements made about processes of nature according to their sensible appearance, even when they "contradict the findings of contemporary scientific knowledge" are "none the less true". Whether this assertion is admissible without further qualification is questionable, unless, indeed, it is intended to introduce the concept of a 'double' truth.

---

[6] Diekamp-Jüssen, *Katholische Dogmatik,* vol. I, pp. 41 f.

This, however, is unnecessary. For in the last analysis there can be no question of distinguishing between the two ways of knowing nature, as though they were two contrasting modes of cognition on the same plane, one as much justified as the other. It cannot be excluded *a priori* that a judgment about a natural process formulated according to imaginative or popular modes of apprehension may be false, just as a statement of natural science can be false when an error has crept in in the manner in which it is formulated. It has to be borne in mind that from the scientific point of view not every figurative mode of expression can be considered as contrary to scientific knowledge; men receive various kinds of knowledge from poetry and everyday experience of the world, and these kinds of knowledge are to be viewed in the context of the sum total of worldly experience.[7] In this context to play off everyday experience against scientific experience is a proceeding which cannot be recommended.

We cannot, then, point to any evident reasons either in Scripture itself or in the tradition of the Church for holding that biblical inerrancy is extended to statements concerned with the field of natural science as well. This being the case, it no longer occasions us any difficulty today to find that conclusions in the Bible concerning natural processes sometimes contain erroneous views. Thus M. Schmaus maintains "the supernatural revelation of God, which comes to us as the written word of God in Scripture, is not meant to give us any information concerning the nature of things. Insofar as nature does appear as the subject of the written word of God, it is not its essence, its activities or its processes that are under discussion. There is no intention of describing nature here as it would be described in natural science.

---

[7] The question of how scientific and non-scientific views of nature are related to one another is the cause of tensions in current thought. As a result of the advances which human knowledge has made this question is conditioned by a sense of microcosm and macrocosm. On this see A. Portmann, "Die Ordnungen des Lebendigen im Deutungsversuch der Biologie", *Eranos-Jahrbuch* 30 (1962), pp. 285–332.

So far from this, the concern of Scripture is to give testimony of that relationship which nature bears to God as Creator and to Christ as Redeemer. The Scriptures also give testimony of that glory to which, as Christ promised, nature will attain, and the revelation of which she eagerly awaits (Rom 8:18–22). In the biblical descriptions of nature, therefore, Scripture is not competing with natural science. They pertain not to that truth which Scripture was intended to communicate, but to the form in which it is presented. Their function is to clothe and to embody revelation. In this process statements may be made about nature which do not conform to the real facts as ascertained by science, but which are based rather upon mere sensible appearances which are in conformity with popular modes of presentation or give expression to the ancient conception of the world. But the inerranc of Scripture is not imperilled by this fact."[8]

By the standards of what is nowadays accepted as common knowledge, then, it is not possible to ascribe inerrancy to Scripture in its statements about nature. This fact immediately raises the question whether the same applies to the historical statements in Scripture. Let us read what M. Schmaus, to take one example, has to say on this point: "The historical statements in the Bible cannot be reduced to the status of literary forms in the same way as statements about the order of nature and its processes (cf. *Spiritus Paraclitus*). For since revelation represents both a way back to Christ and at the same time the way to him, the historical statements which it contains have a different significance from those concerned with nature. They assure us that revelation is an historical fact. Yet even here, according to a decree of the Biblical Commission dated 23rd June 1905 (*D* 1980) there are reliable grounds for accepting the fact that the biblical author does not present us with true history in the strict sense; his purpose is, rather, to impart religious instruction in the form of history. The fact that on many historical matters the information provided in

---

[8] M. Schmaus, *Katholische Dogmatik,* vol. I, pp. 129 f.

Scripture must be regarded as imperfect should not lead us to deny that inerrancy which is ascribed to it in the doctrinal statements of the Church."[9]

It must be admitted that the question of whether historical errors are to be found in the Bible is more complex than that which is concerned with the conclusions of the natural sciences and their relation to Scripture. Here again, however, it is possible, in the last analysis, to make an analogous application of Augustine's principle to the effect that God did not wish to instruct us concerning nature. The Lord in the gospel never gave any kind of promise that he would send the Holy Ghost in order to inform us about the courses of the sun and moon. For the Lord wished to form us as Christians, not to inform us by giving us scientific knowledge of nature: "Non legitur in evangelio Dominum dixisse, Mitto vobis Paracletum qui vos doceat de cursu solis et lunae. Christianos enim facere volebat, non mathematicos."[10]

In the same way it cannot be deduced from Scripture that it was written in order to bequeath to posterity a history of the Jewish people that was exact, perfect and free from error. Faith in God cannot depend upon the question of whether any historical errors of a secondary nature are to be found in a book written by a human hand. Errors of this kind do not impugn those statements in the book which are claimed to be true.[11] No sensible person

---

[9] *Ibid.,* pp. 130 f.

[10] Augustine, *De actis cum Felice Manichaeo* I, X, *PL,* XLII, col. 525.

[11] P. Zerafa, "The Limits of Biblical Inerrancy", pp. 103 f., argues against A. Barucq–H. Cazelles, *Introduction à la Bible,* vol. I (2nd ed., 1959), pp. 61–65, that it is theologically unjustifiable to confine the truth of the Bible to supernatural truths: "This general limitation of inerrancy to a pre-determined biblical object can hardly be backed by any theological justification. St. Thomas follows the lead of St. Augustine in excluding the fashioning of the heavenly bodies from the object of the Bible, but he does not present this restriction as a general principle. He gives only one limitation: God reveals to the prophets what is necessary for the instruction of the faithful. But the extension of this doctrine cannot be established beforehand", *ibid.,* p. 104. On the justification for this objection cf. pp. 87 f. In this connection it must be emphasized that

would condemn a modern historical work as untrue and unhistorical merely because, for instance, it revealed a few errors of style. To do this would be to 'throw the baby out with the bathwater' and, so far as the human element is concerned, would demand something that could not be fulfilled.

Applying this to Scripture, it means that it is exaggerated to infer from an error in a book of the Bible that this involves a contradiction in the Bible itself. The reasoning here would be that if there is an error it must be attributed to God, who cannot lie. But this conclusion would be valid only if Scripture were the word of God in the sense that God had revealed this book direct to a prophet through the mediation of angels, and had not had this book written by men who were subject to error. This is in fact how Mohammedans think of the Koran.[12]

It was thought that a new way had been found of upholding the inerrancy of Scripture in all its historical statements; in explaining the meaning of the biblical books one could have recourse to the *genera litteraria,* literary *genres.* Since the time when this method of explaining Scripture first met with opposition in Catholic circles and was rejected as erroneous[13] allusions to the literary *genres* in current discussion often give the impression that the question of inerrancy can be solved simply by taking due cognizance of them. Thus for instance K. Rahner writes: "What is 'error', for instance, and what is not cannot be defined as easily as it might seem and as one takes for granted. The exegete may mean by 'error', such as he allows to be present somewhere in the New Testament, something that, put differently, covers a true and undeniable

it is not any kind of restriction upon inspiration that is spoken of; all that is called in question is that an 'ideal of perfection' which is foreign to Scripture can justifiably be applied to it.
[12] Cf. H. A. R. Gibb, "Pre-Islamic Monotheism in Arabia", *HTR* 55 (1962), p. 269. On this point Gibb remarks: ". . . Islam, like the other monotheistic religions, is faced with the necessity of reinterpreting the no longer tenable mediaeval concepts of revelation."
[13] Cf. A. Bea, *DBS* 4 (1949), p. 146, on F. v. Hummelauer.

content. This no theologian must or will deny, any more than the Papal encyclicals which exclude all error in Scripture. The exegete gives this qualified meaning to the fact that the verse of Scripture which says that Abiathar (Mk 2:26) was high priest when David ate the loaves of proposition is in 'error'. But this it is only when the verse is read apart from its context, the literary form of the writing, and when it is detached from the frame of reference in which it was uttered and read in isolation — all of which the exegete has the right to do."[14]

Is not this to strain the concept of the literary *genre* quite beyond what it is capable of bearing, by requiring it, namely, to make an error cease to be an error any longer? On the one hand a literary mode of presentation, which is not meant of itself to offer historical information, is not affected by errors contained in it. But on the other hand it cannot perform the feat oft transforming error into accuracy. In other words, when the presence of an historical error can be ascertained, for instance in one of Shakespeare's plays, the play as such does not lose its value thereby, and neither is the error altered by the fact of being included in the plot of the play. All that a correct understanding of the literary *genre* of a text can do is to guard against the danger of interpreting a text completely falsely, and of ascribing some idea to the author which he never intended to express. But whether an author erred in employing a particular *genus litterarium* in dealing with particular topics is a question apart. The problem of the inerrancy of Scripture cannot be solved on the basis of literary *genre*.[15]

[14] K. Rahner in H. Vorgrimler, ed., *Dogmatic versus Biblical Theology* (1964), p. 40. Here the Augustinian line of argument would have to be resumed.

[15] P. Zerafa, *The Limits of Biblical Inerrancy,* p. 101: "An honest appraisal of the biblical message arrived at through the study of the literary forms eliminates those difficulties that flow from a faulty interpretation to the text itself. But this principle cannot be given as a cure-all in matters of inerrancy. Pius XII has not presented it as the primary rule for defending the truth of the Bible; it is just a principle of interpretation, a means of attaining the literal sense ... In this way 'many difficulties' can be solved because 'not infrequently'

The methods so far described are incapable of helping us any further in the task of solving the problem 'In what sense is Scripture free from error?' Perhaps we should conclude, therefore, that we are here confronted with one of those cases in which a biblical concept has become unintentionally combined in the tradition of the Church with a mode of presentation that is ultimately foreign to it. Indeed it is the mode of presentation that has actually come to stand in the foreground. To what extent this has, in actual fact, been the case with regard to scriptural inerrancy must be examined in greater detail in the pages which follow.

Even in dealing with this problem of scriptural inerrancy one must, according to universally recognized theological principles, proceed from the assumption that the Church preserves and defends unimpaired the tradition which has been transmitted to her in Scripture.

Admittedly there is an unresolved question here concerning the documents of the Church's tradition, in which the task of defending the Bible against false charges is carried on. To what extent are these documents, with their justifiable concern to ward off errors, conditioned by opinions and modes of presentation that belong to a particular period, and therefore not to be identified with that which they rightly defend, revelation itself? Even in the case of the inerrancy of Scripture the Church's documents concerning the truth of the Bible are subject to the same rules of interpretation which apply to all ecclesiastical documents. It is therefore matter for investigation how far the ideas connected with the defence of scriptural inerrancy are associated with concerns which were justified at a particular period and with language which was conditioned by that period without belonging to revelation itself. For the special problem of the inerrancy of Scripture, therefore, a proposition of H. Haag's likewise has a

apparent inaccuracies are only the result of special literary forms peculiar to the ancients." N. Lohfink remarks upon this in *Die Irrtumslosigkeit: Das Siegeslied am Schilfmeer* (1965), pp. 44–80.

special relevance. It is formulated in the following terms: "It cannot be contested that [this] manner [previously treated of] of employing concepts of revelation in different senses in the Bible and in ecclesiastical documents leads to tensions. Indeed I may even venture to suggest that at present this is proving the most intractable problem for the relationship of exegesis to dogmatic theology."[16]

What course are we to follow in order to solve this problem? If theology is correct in asserting that the word of God is free from error, then in the first instance it is to the Bible itself that we must put the question: In what sense does it claim to be true? For it can hardly be supposed that the Church is upholding the truth of Scripture in a sense which is quite foreign to what Scripture itself means by *truth*.[17] The method which we shall be using in the pages which follow, therefore, is that of investigating the modes of conception and understanding that are peculiar to the Bible in their bearing upon the concept of truth. Only when we have established what sort of truth the Bible lays claim to can we verify whether this does actually apply to it, and whether the Bible is indeed true in that sense of 'true' which is found in the Bible itself. A further question will then arise, whether that which is described as true in the Bible is also true in our sense, that is according to our concept of truth.[18]

---

[16] H. Haag, "Zum Verhältnis Exegese — Dogmatik", *TQ* 142 (1962), p. 7.
[17] There are no compelling reasons for assuming that the Church draws support for her defence of the inerrancy of Scripture from any 'oral tradition'.
[18] B. Brinkmann writes in *Ph Th* 1 (1966), pp. 117 f.: "In spite of all the author's efforts to find that the source of the inerrancy of Scripture is the covenant faithfulness of God, he fails to carry conviction because the arguments he puts forward are based upon a false premiss. This is the author's failure to distinguish between the inerrancy of Scripture and the inerrancy (= faithfulness) of God, which is recorded in Scripture. For the latter can be established only when it has already been established that Scripture itself does not err in its account of it." What B. Brinkmann is overlooking here is that he himself has fallen into manifold error for 1) What I was referring to was not the inerrancy of Scripture at all, but its truth, and 2) I am not speaking of

The Hebrew word *'emet,* generally rendered in our language as 'truth', is translated in Gesenius-Buhl's Hebrew dictionary in the following manner: "1. Firmness, faithfulness ... peace and security, Jer 33:6 ... 2. Reliability, certainty, sureness ... Josh 2:12, 'a sure sign' ... 'a sure way', Gen 24, 48 ... 'Genuine seed' Jer 2:21 ... 3. As a moral quality: Reliability, integrity, faithfulness: of Yahweh ... (2 Chron 32:1: proof of faithfulness), of a king ... reliable men ..., 'city of faithfulness' of Jerusalem ... God is an *'ēl 'emet,* Ps 31:6, his law *'emet,* Ps 19:10 ... therefore: to walk in God's *'emet,* ..., frequently with *hesed; hesed w'-'emet* love and faithfulness ... of God ... of a king ... *'emet* in faithfulness, upright ... also: 'really', 'in truth' ... 4. In connection with facts which have been narrated: truth = ... true religion Dan 8:12; 9:13."[19]

The meanings given in Gesenius-Buhl for *'emet* are in essence correct,[20] and they are sufficient to enable us to realize that the

the inerrancy of God, which B. Brinkmann, in a wholly unbiblical manner, identifies with God's faithfulness. The objections of K. H. Schelkle (*TQ* 145, pp. 362f.) could be answered on similar lines.

[19] *GB* 52; s. v. *'emet;* cf. also *GB* 47 on *'emūnāh.*

[20] Cf. F. Zorell, *Lexicon Hebraicum et Aramaicum* (1940ff.), p. 67. On *'emet* in the Old Testament see L. Bach, "Der Glaube nach der Anschauung des AT", *Beitr. zur Förderung der christl. Theologie* IV/6 (1900); G. A. Dächsel, *Treue-Verhältnisse im AT. Eine biblisch-rechtliche Studie,* dissertation for Univ. of Breslau (1914); G. Quell, *TWNT,* vol. I, pp. 233–7; W. Staerk, "Der getreue Gott", *ThBl* 16 (1937), pp. 228–34; F. Asensio, *Misericordia et Veritas. El hèsed y 'ēmet divinos, su influjo religioso-social en la historia de Israel* (1949); I. de la Potterie, "De sensu vocis *'emet* in Vetere Testamento", *VD* 27 (1949), pp. 336–54; id. in *VD* 28 (1950), pp. 29–42; I. C. C. van Dorssen, *De Derivate van de Stamm 'amen in het Hebreuwsch van het OT,* dissertation for Univ. of Amsterdam (1951); P. Michalon, "La foi, rencontre de Dieu et engagement envers Dieu, selon l'AT", *NRT* 75 (1953), pp. 587–600; J. H. Vrielink, *Het waarheidsbegrip* (1956); S. Porúbcan, "La radice *'mn* nel AT", *Rivista Biblica* 8 (1960), pp. 324–69; *ibid.* (1961), pp. 173–83, 221–34; A. Weiser, "Glauben im AT" in *Glaube und Geschichte im AT* (1961), p. 334. On *'emet* in Qumran see A. Vögtle, "'Die Wahrheit' als geoffenbarte göttliche Wirklichkeit und wirkende Gotteskraft" in *Oberrheinisches Pastoralblatt* 62 (1961),

senses which are uppermost are 'firmness, stability, reliability, certainty, sureness, integrity, faithfulness'.[21]

The concept of truth found among other Semitic peoples in the ancient Near East is in agreement with this one. For example in Akkadian, however different the actual word is, the concept remains the same as here.[22] Concerning the Semitic and ancient Near Eastern concept of truth, therefore, it could be said: "for the Babylonians and Assyrians, as for the Israelites, truth was something quite different, namely that which endures or, to put it another way, that which has permanence and stability throughout all change. The opposite of truth as conceived of here was not untruth in the sense of statements failing to correspond to facts, but instability, changeability, that which has no real permanence and which, as understood in the ancient Near East, could not be 'true' for that reason."[23]

The conclusion of the foregoing observations is that the Old

---

pp. 3 f.; J. de Caevel, "La connaissance religieuse dans les hymnes de grâces de Qumran", *ETL* 38 (1962), pp. 437, 443; F. Nötscher, "'Wahrheit' als theologischer Terminus in den Qumran-Texten" in *Vom Alten zum Neuen Testament* (1962), pp. 112–25.

[21] I. de la Potterie in *VD* 28 (1950), p. 42: "Vocis *emeth* sensus fundamentalis est firmitas et stabilitas. Haec tamen significatio plerumque manifestatur in ideis constantiae, fidelitatis et veritatis, cum variis aspectibus . . ."

[22] Cf. *AHW*, p. 481, on *kinu* — 'enduring, true, faithful', pp. 494 f., *kittu* I — 'Steadfastness, truth, fidelity'. The example of Hebrew *'emet* and Akkadian *kinu/kittu* I shows very clearly that the same idea can be expressed by two different words, and that for this reason it is methodologically false to conclude that from the lack of parallels for Hebrew *'emet* that it stands for a concept of truth that is peculiar to Hebrew. For the Hebrew concept of truth corresponds to that held by other Semites of the ancient Near East. On the problem of the connection between language and thought cf. A. Marty (cited by H. Arens, *Sprachwissenschaft* [1955], pp. 386 ff.) and J. Barr, *The Semantics of Biblical Language* (1961), pp. 161 ff. ('Faith' and 'Truth' — an Examination of Some Linguistic Arguments).

[23] W. von Soden, "Biblische und geschichtliche Wahrheit", *Amt und Gemeinde* 7 (1956), p. 106. In *ZKT* 87 (1965), p. 198, E. Gutwenger holds that when a distinction is drawn between the Greek concept of truth and the biblical and

Testament speaks in the first instance of God being 'true' to his words, and not of the truth of the words themselves. Certainly the Old Testament does also state that God speaks the truth, that his words are true (cf. 2 Sam 7:28;[24] the New Testament speaks of the true or 'right' utterance, e.g. Mt 5:37; Eph 4:25). The wisdom teachers also show themselves eager to call the law *truth* (Mal 2:6; Prov 8:7–11; 22:17–21),[25] and in the Book of Daniel the revelations of God are also described as 'true', the law is called 'truth', and even the monotheistic religion of Israel, as opposed to that of the Gentiles, is described as 'truth' Dan 8:12).[26]

But for the Old Testament the 'truth' of God is primarily bound up with his faithfulness. Yahweh is the covenant God who not only demands faithfulness from his people but promises to be faithful himself as well.[27] Even when the idea that is uppermost is that God's words are true, still no passage can be pointed to which asserts of Scripture itself that as the word of God it cannot

---

Semitic one this amounts to "... debarring the Semites and Israelites from the species *homo sapiens*". This may apply to an *a priori* approach, but not to modern research into the real position based on historical and philological grounds.

[24] I. de la Potterie (*VD* 28 [1950], pp. 37 f.) believes that Ps 119:43 can also be adduced in this connection, but cf. the cautious observations of A. Deissler, *Psalm 119 (118) und seine Theologie* (1955), pp. 142 f. On the prayer of the suppliant "Take not away the word of truth utterly out of my mouth..." Deissler remarks: "The association of *dābār* and *'emet* occurs once more in v. 160, and also in Ps 15:2. It is a frequent usage in the rest of the Old Testament. A 'word of truth' is one which has something real to which it corresponds. Our psalmist would like to make his opponent aware 'of it' — that is, here, of the visible support of Yahweh." (*Ibid.*, p. 143.) On Ps 119:160, "The sum of thy word is truth" Deissler writes: "As the second stych shows, *'emet* here has much in common with the German term for truth, 'Wahrheit'. Constantia of PP. therefore touches upon the essence of the concept, admittedly at the cost of the connotations which the Hebrew word bears." (*Ibid.*, p. 252.)

[25] I. de la Potterie in *VD* 28 (1950), pp. 38 f.

[26] *Ibid.*, pp. 39 f.

[27] Cf. *BF*, pp. 23 f.; I. de la Potterie in *VD* 27 (1949), pp. 340–50; F. Ascensio, *Misericordia et Veritas* (1949), pp. 197–249 (El *'emet* divino y la idea de pacto).

contain any error. Such a line of thought must necessarily have been quite foreign to the Hebrew tradition, which spoke in the first instance of God's covenant faithfulness.

Later Judaism took over the concept of truth as found in the writings of the Old Testament and developed it further,[28] thereby providing a bridge from the Old Testament to the New. As in the Old Testament, so also in the New ἀλήθεια,[29] the word most often used to translate 'emet,[30] needs to be rendered in different ways. Here too ἀλήθεια is not to be translated 'truth' in all passages.[31] In several passages it means *truthfulness, reliability,*

---

[28] F. Nötscher, '"Wahrheit' als theologischer Terminus in den Qumran-Texten" in *Vom Alten zum Neuen Testament* (1962), pp. 112–25; J. Gnilka, "Wahrheit", *HthG*, vol. II, p. 796.

[29] On ἀλήθεια in the New Testament and in Greek cf. F. Büchsel, *Der Begriff Wahrheit in dem Evangelium und den Briefen des Johannes* (1911); A. Schlatter, *Der Glaube im Neuen Testament* (4th ed., 1927), pp. 551, 599; H. v. Soden, "Was ist Wahrheit?" (1927), newly published in *Urchristentum und Geschichte. Gesammelte Aufsätze und Vorträge*, vol. I (1951), pp. 1–24; R. Bultmann, "Untersuchungen zum Johannesevangelium", *ZNW* 27 (1928), pp. 113–63; G. Quell, G. Kittel and R. Bultman, ἀλήθεια, *TWNT*, vol. I, pp. 233–51; W. Luther, "Der frühgriechische Wahrheitsgedanke im Lichte der Sprache", *Gymnasium* 65 (1958), pp. 75–107; K. Alanen, "Das Wahrheitsproblem in der Bibel und in der griechischen Philosophie", *KD* 3 (1957), pp. 230–9; H. Boeder, "Der frühgriechische Wortgebrauch von Logos und Aletheia", *Archiv für Begriffsgeschichte* 4 (1959), pp. 82–112; A. Vögtle, "'Die Wahrheit' als geoffenbarte göttliche Wirklichkeit und wirkende Gotteskraft", pp. 1–8; E. Heitsch, "Die nicht-philosophische ΑΛΗΘΕΙΑ", *Hermes* 90 (1962), pp. 24–33; id., "Wahrheit als Erinnerung", *Hermes* 91 (1963), pp. 36–52; A. Schwan, "Politik als 'Werk der Wahrheit'" in P. Engelhardt, ed., *Sein und Ethos* (1963), pp. 69–110; K. H. Volkmann–Schluck, "Ethos und Wissen in der Nikomachischen Ethik des Aristoteles" in P. Engelhardt, ed., *Sein und Ethos* (1963), pp. 62 ff.; S. Aalen, "'Truth', a Key Word in St. John's Gospel", *Studia Evangelica* II, *Texte und Untersuchungen*, vol. 87 (1964), pp. 3–24; J. Becker, *Das Heil Gottes. Heil- und Sündenbegriffe in den Qumrantexten und im Neuen Testament* (1964), pp. 176–80, 217–37.

[30] Cf. J. Barr, *The Semantics of Biblical Language*, pp. 187 ff.

[31] Cf. the brief summary in J. Gnilka, *HthG*, vol. II, pp. 796 ff.; I. de la Potterie, *Studiorum Paulinorum Congressus Internationalis Catholicus, 1961,* vol. II (1963), p. 45.

84

uprightness. God is reliable (cf. Rom 3:7[32] because he stands by his promises. 'Truth' means, amongst other things, firmness (Gal 2:5), and, in the context of the vicissitudes of life, 'straightforwardness' (Gal 2:14). In the context of statements being true ἀλήθεια is the opposite of lying (cf. Rom 9:1; 2 Cor 12:6; 1 Tim 2:7; Eph 4:25; James 3:14). As the New Testament sees it, the Christian witness to faith is absolute truth. Thus the apostle calls the gospel the 'word of truth' (Col 1,15; cf. James 1:18). As opposed to erroneous teaching ἀλήθεια is the true, the correct teaching (1 Tim 6:5; 2 Tim 3:8). Ἀλήθεια also designates the 'real state of affairs, the reality' which is the opposite of what appears to be the case (Rom 2:2; 1 Jn 3:18; 2 Jn 1; 3 Jn 1).

The concept of truth in the Fourth Gospel, in which elements from the Old Testament and from the Greek environment alike have been taken up[33] has many different levels of significance in its composition. The essential meaning of ἀλήθεια is determined by the fact that it is applied to the Person of Jesus Christ.[34] Jesus identifies himself with the truth (Jn 14:6). As ἀλήθεια he is the manifestation of the Father, and thereby of the divine life: "But for ἀλήθεια as used in the Johannine Gospel the basic meanings of the Greek and Hebrew terms have been united in a new syn-

---

[32] On 'truth' in Paul see, for example, K. Prümm, *Diakonia/Pneumatos,* vol. II, part 2 (1962), pp. 482–8.

[33] On the Johannine concept of truth cf. I. de la Potterie, "L'arrière-fond du thème johannique de vérité", *Studia Evangelica, Texte und Untersuchungen* 73 (1959), pp. 277–94; id. in *NRT* 88 (1966), p. 164; H. Schlier, "Meditationen über den johanneischen Begriff der Wahrheit", *Festschrift für M. Heidegger* (1959), pp. 195–203; W. Thüsing, *Die Erhöhung und Verherrlichung Jesu im Johannesevangelium* (1960), pp. 146–9. J. Blank, "Der johanneische Wahrheitsbegriff", *BZ* 7 (1963), pp. 163–73; S. Aalen, "'Truth', a Key Word in St. John's Gospel"; J. Becker, *Das Heil Gottes. Heil- und Sündenbegriffe in den Qumrantexten und im Neuen Testament,* pp. 176–80, 217–37.

[34] In addition to the statements in the Johannine writings it is said in Eph. 4:21 that Jesus is the truth, see I. de la Potterie, *Studiorum Paulinorum Congressus Internationalis Catholicus, 1961,* pp. 48 ff.

thesis. Formally speaking it means here 'that which is unconcealed, and which stands firm as the right and the valid'. The original Word that is God lets the gift of 'enlightened' life appear as the 'revealed-and-enduring' and as 'the valid-and-right'."[35]

From the observations so far put forward the following conclusion may be drawn: in no passage do either the Old or the New Testaments claim to be a collection of books that are free from error. The ultimate and basic reasons for this state of affairs are these: — first, in Semitic thought the opposite of the concept of 'truth' is not inerrancy but lying, that which 'shifts its position'.[36] The second reason is that because of their concept of truth the problem that arises in the first instance for the Israelites is whether God is *faithful, reliable*. Sacred Scripture, therefore, is a book that records God's faithfulness to Israel, and according to its own way of understanding it could only be regarded as erroneous, false, untrue if what was recorded, namely the faithfulness of God to the covenant, was a lie — if it said that God had broken his covenant. Here too we must call to mind an observation of von Soden's concerning the Semitic concept of truth: "The concept which is the opposite of this [the Semitic and Israelite concept of truth] was not 'untruth' in the sense of a lack of correspondence between statements and facts, but instability, mutability, that which had no real permanence, and for this reason could not, to ancient Near Eastern eyes, be regarded as true. To seek after this truth was a religious duty for the Babylonians as well as for the Israelites, and not to seek after it was a sin, because it was contrary to the commandment of God or, in the case of Babylon and Assur, the gods who were believed in there . . . It was no contravention of this truth if in the course of historical narratives the author gave a little rein to his fantasies, artificially combined differ-

---

[35] H. Schlier, "Meditationen über den johanneischen Begriff der Wahrheit", p. 195.

[36] On lying in the Old Testament see M. A. Klopfenstein, *Die Lüge nach dem Alten Testament* (1964), pp. 321 f.

ent episodes or added a little embellishment to tradition here and there. Nor was the author considered to have abandoned the way of truth if he set the historical narratives or stories which had come down to him in a context of his own creating, provided that this was in accordance with the knowledge of divine truth that had been given him. When, therefore, we assert or believe that we have observed that biblical stories are not altogether exact in many of their details, or that they are interwoven with elements of legend, anachronisms or human interpretations — for instance of names (so-called popular etymologies), all this does not affect in the very least their truth content as understood in the ancient Near East. Even a narrative which is not exactly in conformity with the facts of history can still be true in this sense, if it bears witness to divine truth in its immutability."[37]

Apart from individual passages in Scripture which say that some word of God is true, 'truth' (*'emet,* ἀλήθεια) is predicated of God in the sense of God being 'faithful' or 'true' to his word, to his promise. God is 'true' inasmuch as he is *faithful* to the covenant with Israel, inasmuch as he puts his word into effect. Regarded from this point of view Scripture is true to the extent it speaks of a God of truth, and Scripture would lie, would be in error if it presented a God who did not keep his word.

When the problem of truth in Scripture is viewed from this aspect it also becomes comprehensible why the Church has always upheld the cause of an unrestricted truth of Scripture. Here too it becomes apparent why the well-meant attempts to save the inerrancy of Scripture by the expedient of restricting that inerrancy solely to the supernatural truths contained in it should fail to satisfy. These efforts proceed from an *a priori* assumption. For the distinction between natural and supernatural has only a limited value[38] and for this reason cannot be applied to the problem of

---

[37] W. von Soden, "Biblische und geschichtliche Wahrheit", pp. 106 f.
[38] Cf. J. Alfaro, *LTK,* vol. VII, cols. 830–35.

scriptural inerrancy without further qualification. According to the Bible itself we should speak of the truth of God as unrestricted and the inerrancy of Scripture is unrestricted for the same reason, because the subject of its message is the faithfulness of God that endures for ever. Since God's faithfulness is revealed in his words and in his deeds, the Church has always included the historical events narrated in the Bible in her defence of scriptural inerrancy. The deeds of salvation performed by God must have taken place, because otherwise God would not have proved or made good his claim to 'truth' (faithfulness). But we would be entertaining a false understanding of truth if we believed that the human presentation of God's salvific deeds must be a record of facts, exact and free from error in every smallest detail. In the case supposed we would be upholding not the truth of Scripture but in place of this Scripture as perfect history writing. This would be to apply the concept of truth that belongs to the Greek and Western history of ideas to Scripture. Whatever justification there may be for this concept (and that is a question that still remains problematical)[39]

---

[39] On the question of truth cf. G. Krüger, *Grundfragen der Philosophie. Geschichte—Wahrheit—Wissenschaft* (1958), pp. 10–23, 73–150, 235–68; E. Zellinger, "Zur Kritik des psychologischen Irrationalismus", *Seelenleben und Menschenbild — Festschrift Ph. Lersch* (1958), p. 189, on the problem of the 'original truth'; H. Blumberg, "Paradigmen zu einer Metaphorologie", *Archiv für Begriffsgeschichte* 6 (1960), pp. 7–142; M. Gabriel, "Sinn und Wahrheit. Aus dem gegenwärtigen Stand der Wahrheitsfrage" in R. Wisser, ed., *Sinn und Sein* (1960), pp. 135–53; M. Heidegger, *Nietzsche*, vol. II, pp. 193 ff.; R. Pflaumer, "Zum Wesen von Wahrheit und Täuschung bei Platon", *Die Gegenwart der Griechen im neueren Denken — H.-G. Gadamer-Festschrift* (1960), pp. 189–224; R. Bilz, "Die Wahrheit in ihrer Beziehung zu Faszination und Verdrängung", *Jahrbuch für Psychologie, Psychotherapie und medizinische Anthropologie* 7 (1960), pp. 243–57; H. Kuhn, "Wahrheit und geschichtliches Verstehen", *HZ* 193 (1961), pp. 376–89; G. Gawlick, "Wahrheit", *RGG* VI (1962), cols. 1518–25; W. Kamlah, "Der moderne Wahrheitsbegriff", *Einsichten, G. Krüger-Festschrift* (1962), pp. 107–30; R. Berlinger, "Das Ereignis der Wahrheit", *Perennitas, Th. Michels-Festschrift* (1963), pp. 538–56; H. Deku, "Was ist Wahrheit?" in M. Schmaus and W. Läpple eds., *Wahrheit und Zeugnis* (1964), pp. 826–33.

it cannot be considered to be equivalent to the biblical and Semitic[40] concept of truth.[41]

If, then, we accept the inerrancy of Scripture in the sense expounded here, in what sort of case could we still say that an error was present in it? Since the truth of God is manifested in his faithfulness to his covenant people, Scripture could only be charged with error if God broke his faith with Israel. But so long as Israel exists, albeit divided into an Israel κατὰ σάρκα and an Israel κατὰ πνεῦμα, God has kept faith with his people, and in that case Scripture can only be accused of lying when *Israel is annihilated.*[42]

If it is in the sense proposed here that Scripture claims to be true, it also becomes clear why the Church holds firm in her belief in the truth of Scripture, and not in its inerrancy (for Vatican II see *Dei Verbum,* Ch. III, art. 11). The truth of Scrip-

---

[40] With reference to the failure to recognize the element which is peculiar to the Semitic concept of truth W. von Soden (*BiOr* 20 [1963], p. 149) remarks: "Apart from this many errors are caused by maintaining a concept of truth which is not in conformity with the Bible."

[41] Attempts of this kind unconsciously lead to false interpretations of statements in the Bible. An assertion by A. Bea, in which he adduces the following argument from the New Testament in support of *perfecta inerrantia* runs as follows: "Absoluta scripturae auctoritas et supponitur et expressis verbis docteur. 'Non potest scriptura solvi' teste Domino (Jn 10:35), 'Ut scriptura impleatur' (Jn 17:12); 'Necesse est impleri omnia quae scripta sunt' (Lk 24:44). Et Alia. Apostolorum dictis et consuetudine idem comprobatur cf. Acts 1:16; Jn 2:17. 22; 12:38 ff.; 19:24, 28, 36; 1 Cor 15:4 et alia permulta, ex quibus apparet secundum persuasionem Apostolorum nihil esse in scriptura quod non verum sit, et ideo quod in scriptura legatur, debeat admitti ut verum." The claim of the Scriptures to be "fulfilled" is here identified with *perfecta inerrantia.* A. Lang (*Fundamentaltheologie,* vol. II [3rd ed., 1962], p. 310) also adduces arguments from Jn 10:35 and Mt 5:18 in support of "an absolute inerrancy of Scripture".

[42] Here let us only touch in passing upon the fact that the question of the existence of Israel as a people has its intellectual and linguistic aspects as well, and that these are no less vital than what we are accustomed to understand as 'faithfulness'. 'Truth' and 'faithfulness' are to be viewed here in the light of their historical contexts.

ture is more than the fact (to be proved as best one can), that a book contains no error. When she gives her unrestricted assent to the complete truth of Scripture the Church is proclaiming her faith in God's faithfulness: "He who calls you is faithful" (1 Thess 5:24).

Since, then, in considering the problem of the truth of Scripture we find that it is inseparably connected with the idea of God's own truth or faithfulness, this conclusion leads to results which have an important bearing on our general attitude to the Bible:

1. The dispute between Galileo and the Inquisition is caused, in the last analysis, by a misunderstanding on the Inquisition's part with regard to the biblical concept of truth. The absolute inerrancy of Scripture, as upheld by the Inquisition[43] is a theological doctrine that has no basis either in sacred Scripture itself or in the tradition of the Church. According to the Bible we have to uphold the truth of God in the sense of his faithfulness but not as providing us with a 'true' representation of the material world.

2. *Truth* and *truths* in Scripture. Since passages are also found in sacred Scripture in which *'emet* and ἀλήθεια are to be translated as 'truth',[44] it might be objected that sacred Scripture knows of our concept of truth also, and that it is therefore impossible to maintain consistently the point of view proposed here. To this it must be replied that Scripture does also contain truths which cannot simply be reduced to the concept of 'faithfulness', or 'firmness'. Instances of this are the uniqueness of God, the creation of the world by God, his knowledge of all things etc.[45] While we

---

[43] On the dispute between Galileo and the Inquisition and the function of the inerrancy of Scripture see Loretz, *Galilei,* pp. 101 ff.

[44] Cf. pp. 84 ff.

[45] L. Alonso-Schökel, *Bib* 46 (1965), p. 379; J. Jensen, *CBQ* 25 (1965), p. 276, raises the same question: "Granted that Scripture does not normally formulate doctrine as we do, does it not teach truths — truths not immediately indentifiable with God's fidelity, not immediately derivable from it — that we must formulate (e. g. the personal nature of the Holy Spirit) and hold as taught inerrantly (even in the Western sense) in Scripture? In fact the Church does so formulate her doctrine, and proclaims them to have been revealed."

cannot, and indeed do not dispute this, we must at the same time observe that sacred Scripture sees these truths in their connection with a single great truth, namely the faithfulness of God to his people. Thus it would have to be shown that Deutero-Isaiah, for instance, still spoke of a 'true' God even when Yahweh was unfaithful to Israel.[46] The ultimate criterion of truth here — and in questions connected with the truth of the Bible it is with the ultimate that we are concerned — is for Israel the faithfulness of God, which will be completely revealed only at the end of history. Each individual 'intellectual' and 'historical' truth contained in the Bible is, viewed in the context of sacred Scripture as a whole, connected with God's faithfulness to his people, and is directed towards its fulfilment, the historical 'making good' of his word by God, which will bring history to its close. With regard to the truth of the Bible, therefore, the question is not, in the first instance, how many individual truths and errors the Bible contains. It is concerned, rather, with the living belief of the Church that the books of Scripture teach without error (biblically expressed this would be without 'lies') that truth which God has willed to set down in it for the sake of our salvation. Precisely in this instance of the problem of the truth of Scripture we should not fasten upon individual points, but take into account scriptural truth as a whole[47] and the end towards which it is directed in history, namely the consummation of revelation which is, at the same time, the consummation of truth in the biblical sense.[48] The nature of the covenant of God with his people is such that no abstract divine truths are revealed. For divine revelation is bestowed on the covenant people and is

---

[46] Cf. W. Zimmerli's fundamentally important article, "Der Wahrheitserweis Jahwes nach der Botschaft der beiden Exilspropheten", *Tradition und Situation — Festschrift A. Weiser* (1963), pp. 150 ff.

[47] *Verbum Dei,* Ch. III, art. 12: ". . . respiciendum est ad contentum et unitatem totius Scripturae."

[48] *Ibid.,* Ch. II, art. 8: "Ecclesia scilicet, volventibus saeculis, ad plenitudinem divinae veritatis iugiter fendit, donec in ipsa consumentur verba Dei."

concerned with their life with God, so that without the existence of this people (a factor which is dependent upon the faithfulness of God to Israel) every 'truth' would *ipso facto* become a lie. This is the manner in which the thought develops in sacred Scripture. It is not abstract or systematic.

3. Our attitude to the Semitic and biblical concept of truth. A problem which radically affects this arises from the fact that by our methods it is quite possible either to verify or to reveal the inaccuracy of particular details recorded in the Bible. If, however, we view sacred Scripture as a whole, our present situation is such as to make us incapable either of finally verifying it or of finally disproving it. The ultimate decision awaits the fulfilment which is to come at the end of the ages. Moreover, the truth that is found in sacred Scripture is not something over which man can arbitrate as supreme judge. The problem of truth in the Bible, therefore, is shown to have certain points in common with the problem of truth in science.[49]

4. The term 'inerrancy of sacred Scripture' (inerrantia scripturae) should be dropped. It is sufficient to speak of the truth of Scripture. The 'tower of Babel'-like confusion of terms in this context still persists in spite of Vatican II. Thus, for instance, A. Grillmeier, *ThPh* 1 (1966), p. 179, writes on *Dei Verbum:* "Here it is a question rather of recapturing the great perspectives and the proper sense of scriptural inerrancy." It would probably be more in accordance with *Dei Verbum* to say that in the Constitution it is a question of recapturing the proper sense of the truth of Scripture.

5. The relationship between the truth of the Bible and the canon of biblical books. If, then, the Bible is the book of the covenant people of the Old and New Testaments, recording the 'true-ness' (in the sense of faithfulness) of God and Israel on the

---

[49] The *Wissenschaft und Weisheit* symposium shows very clearly that science does not consist simply in the possession of truth, but is rather on the way to attaining it.

one hand, and the faithlessness of men on the other, then it can be, at basis, only an indication, an imperfect account of the living bond between God and his people. Thus the writings of the Bible cannot perfectly reflect that of which they speak, any more than life can be transformed into ink on a page.

It is from this that the problem of the canon arises. Viewing this problem from a different angle P. Schütz has accurately expressed it as follows: "Hence that in the canon which is untenable — it is that, nevertheless, that must be held; the element of contradiction in its various parts, in spite of which they do cohere; the element of chance in the way in which it has been drawn up, daunting as it indeed is — and yet its survival as *summa summarum!* Its utterly temporary and provisory nature as an accumulation of shortcomings, a true *confusio hominum* — and yet in the midst of the confusion the capital letter of a script written by no earthly hand, intermingled with letters that have run wild! For this reason earlier readers have found it possible to say that the language of the Bible appears as some kind of 'glossolalia in the grand style'. The bold compression of its elements would on this analogy be understood as pertaining to its openness — the freedom of God himself, who speaks in it, and tells us impossible things. It is the language that says 'what is to happen in the future'; it does not, like all other languages, merely say what lies in the past and — touching upon what is, perhaps, still more uncertain — the present. The prophetic word is expressed in it, and it is the language that carries high explosive in it; for it is the future that the Spirit will announce (Jn 16:13)."[50]

Turning from this viewpoint let us now consider the canon.

Vatican II. Vital for the problem with which we are concerned is Ch. III, art. 11: "Therefore, since everything asserted by the inspired authors or sacred writers must be held to be asserted by the Holy Spirit, it follows that the books of Scripture must be

[50] P. Schütz, *Parusia* (1963), p. 576.

93

acknowledged as teaching firmly, faithfully and without error, that truth that God wanted to put into the sacred writings for the sake of our salvation."

In this important passage the theological theory that sacred Scripture is *sine ullo errore* is dropped; thereby the concept of truth associated with this theory is also abandoned.[51] The truth spoken of in this passage is to be understood as truth in the biblical sense: the Bible records for the people of the Old and New Testaments the covenant which God made, and what he said and did; it claims that its account of all this is true in the Semitic sense, i.e. that God has worked, is working and will work for the salvation of man. Stated negatively the same thing might by formulated as follows: — Scripture does not deceive us with regard to our salvation. How far the individual statements of Scripture, viewed in isolation, are 'true' or 'false' in our sense of the terms

---

[51] For an account of the way in which *Dei Verbum* came to be written, and of the overthrow of the *sine ullo errore* theory see Loretz, *Galilei,* p. 182–209. As used in *Dei Verbum,* Ch. III, art. 11, the phrase *sine errore* should probably be understood as equivalent in biblical terms to 'without lying'. The distinction which Scripture draws is between truth and lying. B. Brinkmann (*PhTh* 1 [1966], p. 118) holds that "the most that can be said is that Scripture testifies without error to the covenant faithfulness of God". This statement is misleading, for sacred Scripture does contain errors, but does not lie regarding the faithfulness of God. Brinkmann also writes: *(ibid.)* "In connection with the form in which this message is embodied, subject as this is to temporal limitations, God wills not to make any absolute statements, but permits the hagiographers to express themselves, under the influence of the Holy Spirit, according to their own ideas (which are not immune to error), or according to the views prevailing at the time when they wrote. Thus all that God says here is that 'this is the situation' as the hagiographers conceive of it, or as seen through the eyes of their contemporaries. Here too, therefore, no error is being maintained." Again at this point, then, it must be said that this statement by B. Brinkmann turns out to be fundamentally at variance with *Dei Verbum.* With his conception of the 'absolute assertion' B. Brinkmann shows himself in every way an upholder of a certain philosophical conception of the nature of judgment, and it is this philosophical conception that represents the chief support of the *sine ullo errore* theory which the Council disavows.

is an open question.[52] A further point is that any attempt at combining the question of the truth of the Bible with the problem of literary *genres* is avoided in *Dei Verbum*.

[52] The Council has carefully refrained from giving rules for distinguishing between truth and error. There are fundamental considerations which make this impossible, for the Church cannot take the decision which of the scientific methods is true or false in such a way as to solve finally and for all purposes the question of the truth of Scripture (ch. III, art. 12). In deciding the form in which truth is expressed the *genera litteraria* must be taken into account. This method is applicable to philology as a whole, and not merely to biblical philology.

CHAPTER SIX

THE CANON

In his writings on the canon the Jewish savant M. L. Margolis has said that the usage is Christian, the word Semitic (cf. the Hebrew *gāneh* — reed, cane, measuring stick) and the actual concept Jewish.[1] As a preliminary view of the problem which arises in connection with the canon this statement is particularly serviceable.

Behind the canon lies a long history of development.[2] This is shown, for instance from the fact that as far as the Catholic Church is concerned it was only with the Council of Trent that this history was brought to its conclusion. With good reason, therefore, one writer[3] has remarked of the Tridentine decree on canonicity that it "put a full stop to the thousand-year-old development of the biblical canon".[4] Up to this Council it was still possible to hold divergent views concerning the extent and the precise significance of the canon, these questions being regarded as still not definitively and unambiguously solved.[5] The causes of

---

[1] M. L. Margolis, *La formation de la bible hébraïque* (1953), p. 65.

[2] On the history of the New Testament canon see K. Baus, *From the Apostolic Community to Constantine,* Handbook of Church History, ed. by H. Jedin and J. Dolan, vol. I (1965), pp. 196f.; L. Goppelt, *Die Kirche in ihrer Geschichte,* vol. I, part A (1962), pp. 103–12, § 19.

[3] H. Jedin, *A History of the Council of Trent,* vol. II (1961), p. 91.

[4] The precise reason for speaking only of a thousand-year-old development is not explained.   [5] Cf. *ibid.,* pp. 55f.

this prolonged uncertainty concerning the extent and the nature of the canon are inherent in the canon itself. We have now to enquire how far the canon is derived from the covenant of God with Israel, how far it is based upon the special form of revelation associated with the covenant, and what sort of mutual interrelationship can be found between the two questions of the truth of Scripture and the canon of Scripture.

A necessary part of the sealing of the covenant was the setting down in writing of the covenant obligations.[6] Here, right at the outset, then, we find a written document recognized as a part of the covenant. Any attitude of hostility to the written word is thereby excluded from the very outset.[7]

A further factor which derives from the nature of the covenant is the division of the Old Testament writings into three main parts, namely law, history and that written tradition which was developed in the course of Israel's history by prophets, scribes and priests.[8] For it was these classes which set themselves to explain the meaning of her law and her history. The law constitutes a major part of Old Testament literature. Since the acceptance of God's will and law constituted the central point in the whole episode of the making of the covenant[9] it was inevitable that law should be accorded a central place.[10] Then, to meet altered cir-

---

[6] Cf. *BF,* pp. 26 f., 38 ff.

[7] This is not to dispute the existence of oral tradition in Israel. It must be borne in mind, however, that the world in which Israel lived was 'writing-prone'. The accounts of the use of oral tradition in Israel have so far been unsatisfactory, cf. R. C. Culley, "An Approach to the Problem of Oral Tradition", *VT* 13 (1963), pp. 113–25. The position adopted by this writer represents an advance on the previous discussion of the problem.

[8] R. B. Y. Scott, "Priesthood, Prophecy, Wisdom, and the Knowledge of God", *JBL* 80 (1961), pp. 1–15; P. Grelot, "L'Inspiration scripturaire", *RScR* 51 (1963), pp. 350 ff., uses the expression *charismes fonctionnels* in his treatment of the problem.

[9] Cf. *BF,* pp. 31, 38 ff.

[10] On Law in the Old Testament cf. W. Zimmerli, "Das Gesetz im Alten Testament", *TLZ* 85 (1960), pp. 481–98; id., *Das Gesetz und die Propheten*

cumstances, law had necessarily to be adapted. After the transition from the wilderness to the cultivated land of Canaan it became necessary to take up some sort of positive attitude towards the laws of the new land. Israel was compelled to come to terms with this world, and to absorb whatever could be reconciled with the spirit of the covenant. The element of written legal tradition grew incessantly, and apart from this development, which must be regarded as the outcome of sheer necessity, law also became the subject of meditation and, in the post-exilic community, assumed an ever-increasing importance with the result that it thrust history into the background.[11] The law given to Israel at Sinai provides a basis both for the subsequent development of further laws and for the literature which grew up about the law. Since Israel had bound herself to uphold the clauses of the covenant for all time, a continual increase in the law was made inevitable. New conditions of life demanded of their very nature that tradition should be both adapted and maintained, and this led to a new written interpretation of the law and to a parenesis[12] which was appropriate to the altered circumstances.

That major part of Israel's written tradition which is historically orientated can be traced back to the covenant in a similar way. The acts of deliverance performed by God in history, above all

(1963); D. Rössler, *Gesetz und Geschichte, Untersuchungen zur Theologie der jüdischen Apokalyptik und der pharisäischen Orthodoxie* (1960); J. J. Stamm, "Dreißig Jahre Dekalogforschung", *ThRu* 27 (1961), pp. 189–239, 281–305; St. Gewirtz, "West-Semitic Curses and the Problem of the Origins of Hebrew Law", *VT* 11 (1961), pp. 137–58; F. C. Fensham, "The Possibility of the Presence of Casuistic Legal Material at the Making of the Covenant at Sinai", *PEQ* 93 (1961), pp. 143–6; A. Kilian, "Apodiktisches und kasuistisches Recht im Licht ägyptischer Analogien", *BZ* 7 (1963), pp. 185–202; id., *Literarkritische und formgeschichtliche Untersuchung des Heiligkeitsgesetzes* (1963).

[11] *BF*, p. 99. In late-Jewish apocalyptic the law is considered to be the "Document of divine election which assembles and unites the community of the saved". See D. Rössler, *Gesetz und Geschichte*, p. 111.

[12] For instance on the developed parenesis of Deuteronomy cf. N. Lohfink, *Das Hauptgebot* (1963), pp. 90 ff.

the exodus from Egypt, are preparations for the making of the covenant and were meant to show the people that they owed obedience to God. For this reason the actual covenant formula is prefaced by an historical summary.[13] In the period which followed Israel was constantly brought back to fresh realizations of the connection between her situation in the present and her own past history; to view her way through the ages from the perspective of the making of the covenant. She sought to understand how Yahweh, her covenant Lord had intervened in the history of his people, and how he had remained true to his covenant. Since Israel had to keep alive the memory of God's acts of salvation on her behalf, she was constantly forced to come to terms with her own history. Thus from the very outset the making of the covenant ensured that history writing would have an important place in Israel.

The making of the covenant took place in the wilderness. It was there that God had actually revealed himself, and there that he had imparted his law. But this does not imply any radical hostility to more sedentary and cultivated ways of life than that of desert nomads. This was the mistake of the Rechabites; they wanted to preserve desert life as an ideal even in the midst of the fertile and cultivated land. But this remained no more than an episode in Israel's history; it could not represent any solution for her.[14] Once she had achieved sedentation in the promised land it was a matter of life and death for Israel to define her position in regard to the higher culture of the Canaanites. The main burden of this struggle was borne by the prophets.[15] The records of Mari enable us to realize that prophetism must have been a widespread phenomenon in the world of that time.[16] In Israel it defended the

[13] Cf. *BF*, pp. 21 f., 98 f.

[14] Jer 35:1–19; W. Rudolph, *Jeremia* (2nd ed., 1958), pp. 207 ff.

[15] W. Baumgartner, "Ugaritische Probleme und ihre Tragweite für das Alte Testament", *TZ* 3 (1947), pp. 81–100.

[16] A. Lods, "Une Tablette inédite de Mari intéressante pour l'histoire ancienne du prophétisme sémitique", *Studies in Old Testament Prophecy* (1957), pp. 103–10;

rights of the covenant against the baals, and did not hesitate to integrate with the covenant ethos all that could be accepted from a culture that was so strongly dominated by the element of sexuality. The prophets upheld the interests of the unique God of Sinai, and while they had to refuse to allow the sexual character of the fertility gods to be ascribed to him, or to let him be represented as having a goddess as his consort, still they did speak of the covenant relationship as a marriage bond, and thus gave some place to the erotic element in the religious sphere.[17] The prophets ceaselessly reproached the faithless people for their disloyalty to the covenant and exhorted them to return to the one God of Israel and to the order willed by him.[18] Subsequently the words of the prophets were preserved and collected as testifying to this spirit.

The 'sages' or 'scribes' also played a part in the shaping of Israel's literary heritage. If Israel was not to remain backward and inferior in the land she had to accept the standards and methods of the only 'university'[19] then available. The world which Israel now entered upon had been accustomed from ancient times to the phenomenon of 'sages' teaching their disciples. Israel took over the 'school' system of these and developed it along lines of her own. Tradition ascribes a decisive role to Solomon in this

W. von Soden, *Die Welt des Orients* I (1950), pp. 397 ff. On the problems raised in current research into the prophetic books see G. Fohrer, "Remarks on Modern Interpretation of the Prophets", *JBL* 80 (1961), pp. 309–19; id., *ThRu* 28 (1962), pp. 1 ff., 235 ff., 301 ff.; S. Herrmann, "Prophetie in Israel und Ägypten. Recht und Grenze eines Vergleichs", *VTS* 9 (1963), pp. 47–65; H. Hirsch, "Prophetismus im Alten Orient", *Bibel und zeitgemässer Glaube* I (1965), pp. 161–9.

[17] Cf. E. Jacob, *Ras Shamra et l'Ancien Testament* (1960), p. 120; O. Loretz, "Die theologische Bedeutung des Hohenliedes", *BZ* 10 (1966), pp. 29–43.

[18] Cf. p. 66.

[19] On the Babylonian 'school' cf. A. Falkenstein, "Die Babylonische Schule", *Saeculum* 4 (1953), pp. 125–37; A. L. Oppenheim, *Ancient Mesopotamia* (1964), pp. 228 ff.

process.[20] It was probably from these schools, where singing and poetry were practised, that the chants sung in the course of the temple liturgy (psalms) were in part derived. It is to these circles too that we owe the so-called 'Wisdom' literature.[21] In the works representative of this literature the sage comes to grips with problems which were traditionally speculated upon at this time (the problem of the justice of God,[22] the Proverbial literature[23]), but in Israel this was undertaken in the spirit of the religion of Yahweh. Since the scribes of this class won high esteem it became impossible for zealots of later ages to exclude certain parts of the Wisdom literature, such as the Song of Solomon and Ecclesiastes, from the literature traditionally recognized.

As literature proliferated in the period before Christ measures were taken to protect the literature of the Old Testament by separating it from that which was recent in origin. The earlier heritage acquired a position of pre-eminence, and was thereby raised to the status of canonical literature. These writings alone were regarded as emanating from the Holy Spirit.[24]

Thus without any exaggeration it can be said that the canonical writings of the Old Testament, both in the outlook which they all have in common and in their diversity, can only be understood when they are viewed against the background of the covenant. The tradition of the Old Testament is extended still further in the

---

[20] Cf. R. B. Y. Scott, "Solomon and the Beginnings of Wisdom in Israel", *VTS* 3 (1955), pp. 262–79.

[21] S. Mowinckel, *VTS* 3 (1955), pp. 206–8.

[22] On the problem of the justice of God among the Semites see W. von Soden in *RGG* 5 (1961), col. 1693.

[23] B. Gemser, *Sprüche Salomos* (1963), pp. 1–4.

[24] Cf. W. Foerster, "Der Heilige Geist im Spätjudentum", *NTS* 8 (1961/62), p. 117, n. 3. On the problem of the development of the canon in detail cf. E. Flesseman van Leer, "Prinzipien der Sammlung und Ausscheidung bei der Bildung des Kanons", *ZTK* 61 (1964), p. 404–18; A. C. Sundberg Jr., "The Protestant Old Testament Canon: Should it be Re-examined?", *CBQ* 28 (1966), pp. 194–203; N. Appel, *Kanon und Kirche. Die Kanonkrise im heutigen Protestantismus als kontroverstheologisches Problem* (1964).

New. In it much space is given to the question of the law.[25] History becomes once more important.[26] The 'prefatory history' of the new covenant is made to extend from the Old Testament to Jesus, and the events of the present are once more seen as an intervention of God in the course of the world's history (cf. Acts 7; 8:2–53; 13:16ff.). The Wisdom tradition too is found to be continued and extended in the doctrinal and instructional sections of the New Testament. All this is finally committed to writing and leads to the formation of the New Testament documents; then these again are separated off as a single body from other writings, to which the Church is compelled to refuse any further inclusion on the grounds that they provide no authentic record of the decisive event.

It is clear from this that the history of God's people, conditioned as it is by the covenant made between Yahweh and Israel, is reflected in the multiplicity of the canonical writings and in the problems to which they give rise. Furthermore in these canonical writings we have before us the literature which was recognized as normative for the people of God.[27]

If, then, the canon is indeed the outcome of a long and chequered history it necessarily follows that the writings contained in it are of varying value. The question then arises of the 'canon within the canon', how the later development in this literature, in which it had fallen away somewhat from its pristine purity, should be distinguished from the original writings. The problem is not new. Different grades (i.e. degrees of authority) among the books of the Bible were referred to at the Council of Trent.[28] However, this problem was abandoned without being pursued any further, although the inequality in value between the various

[25] P. Bläser, "Gesetz", *HthG,* vol. I, pp. 506–14.   [26] *BF,* p. 99, n. 5.
[27] The problem of what forces were brought to bear in the formation of the canon, in order to arrive, for practical purposes, at a recognition of whether a given book should or should not count as normative — this constitutes a question apart.
[28] H. Jedin, *A History of the Council of Trent,* vol. II, pp. 55f.

parts of Scripture has remained a persistent problem.[29] By contrast, in the current discussion between Protestants and Catholics concerning the unequal value of various parts of the canonical writings, the discussion turns upon the question of what is to be cut out of the New Testament as 'early Catholic'.[30] In what sense can we speak of a gradation among the books, or of a 'canon within the canon'? To set the canonical writings side by side as of equal value would be to do violence both to the history of the canon and to its meaning. Who, for instance, would accord the prophet Obadiah equal rank with Isaiah, without making himself absurd? In the New Testament too no-one would declare the Second Epistle of Peter or the Epistle of Jude to be equal in value to (for instance) the Pauline epistles or the Johannine gospel. The inequality of the biblical writings remains a fact. What are the implications of this for the Church?

The final conclusion to be drawn from the multiplicity of writings, ideas and doctrines included in the canon is that it is only by doing violence to the facts that we can identify the revelation of Yahweh with a dogmatic system. The rise and fall of the thoughts and ideas of the Old and New Testaments, the development of the doctrines contained in them, as well as the historical fact that such doctrines sometimes become neglected or ineffective — all this can be discerned in the canonical Scriptures. And what it reveals is, in the first instance, simply that Yahweh has made a covenant with men. God does not demand from those

---

[29] As instances of how this affected the practice of the Church we may recall that e.g. the reading of the Old Testament was forbidden to laymen over a long period. Moreover, those who were obliged to the recitation of the psalms were compelled to put up with their inconsistencies. The problem can hardly be solved by cutting out the passages which are unpopular (cf. E. Bermimont, "De l'inégale valeur des psaumes", *NRT* 84 [1962], pp. 843–52), for this would be to set oneself up as arbiter over the canon as it in fact exists not indeed in theory, but certainly in practice.

[30] Cf. H. Küng, "Der Frühkatholizismus im Neuen Testament als kontroverstheologisches Problem", *TQ* 142 (1962), pp. 385–424; E. Käsemann, "Paulus und der Frühkatholizismus", *ZTK* 60 (1963), pp. 75–89.

belonging to his people that their thoughts should be 'frozen' —
brought to a standstill. Nor does he demand that their thoughts
should be in complete conformity with his, for this is an ideal
that could never be realized. What has to be clung to with the
mind throughout all vicissitudes and fresh beginnings is its basic
assent to what is essential in the covenant, namely a living
fellowship with God, whether this takes the form made possible
by the Old Testament in its period or through Jesus Christ in
the New. It is this striving to keep faith with the covenant Lord
amid fresh difficulties of spirit to which the Old and New Testaments bear witness, and in this respect, working through the
most varied periods, are unanimous, ranging, for instance, from
the sages who were preoccupied with the problem of how the
world came to be from the viewpoint of their faith in Yahweh
(Gen 1 : 1 ff.) to the men who fought to ward off the perils of Gnosti-
cism. In this connection a special question which has been raised
in the discussion of early Catholicism is whether the unity of the
Church is based upon the New Testament canon. In the light
of what has been said above the answer to this question should be
that neither the unity of the Church nor the multiplicity of the
sects has any basis in the unity of the canon. For the canon is
simply the list of those books which are accepted as normative
by the undivided Church. From the point of view of history the
covenant people were there before their books, even though
here again the people was, for its part, conscious from the very
outset of being bound by written documents. But inasmuch as
the one Church accepted the canon as a whole, it made this canon
serve the interests of its own unity. He who acknowledges this
canon is a member of the one Church. Now E. Käsemann, having
established the existence of a certain opposition between Paul
and James in their teaching on justification, and also between
other assertions in the New Testament,[31] comes to the following

[31] E. Käsemann, "Begründet der neutestamentliche Kanon die Einheit der
Kirche?", *Exegetische Versuche und Besinnungen,* vol. I (1960), pp. 220 f., E. T.:
Essays on New Testament Themes, vol. I (1964).

conclusion: "The canon of the New Testament does not as such provide any basis for the unity of the Church. On the contrary, from the evidence which it makes available to the historian, it provides a basis for the multiplicity of the sects."[32] But from what has been said earlier it is clear that what he is here denying to the canon is a function which it has never claimed to exercise. The canon of the Church was developed in the course of defending the Church's unity, and has never been anything more than a touchstone of ecclesiastical unity; it has never provided the basis for that unity. The development of the canon "was achieved in the course of a relentless struggle against the pseudo-gospel".[33] Nevertheless when the Church declared a given document to belong to the canon she thereby recognized it as binding upon herself and as pertaining to her unity. The problem of the gospel within the gospel only arose in the Church from the time of Marcion onwards.[34]

While, therefore, the interpretation of the canon in E. Käsemann's sense is quite without foundation, it has still to be determined whether the solution proposed by H. Küng,[35] in an attempt to deal with the problem which Käsemann raises in this connection, can be justified in all respects. In his discussion of Käsemann's thesis Küng acknowledges that the New Testament canon is indeed that which the multiplicity of the sects *presupposes*[36] (Käsemann's term is 'is based upon'!). This much, Küng believes, must be conceded to Käsemann "for a) there is a diversification of Christian sects, b) the different Christian sects do appeal to the New Testament canon and trace their line of development back to the New Testament, c) these appeals to the New Testament

[32] *Ibid.,* p. 221.
[33] L. Goppelt, *Die Kirche in ihrer Geschichte,* vol. I, part A, p. 112.
[34] F. Mussner, "Evangelium und Mitte des Evangeliums", *Gott in Welt — Festgabe für K. Rahner,* vol. I (1964), p. 507.
[35] H. Küng, "Der Frühkatholizismus im Neuen Testament als kontrovers-theologisches Problem", *TQ* 142 (1962), pp. 385–424.
[36] *Ibid.,* p. 401.

canon, diversified though they are, have a *fundamentum in re,* a basis, that is, in the complexity, multiplicity and inconsistency in theological positions which has been described, and which do exist in the New Testament canon itself. To that extent, then, the New Testament canon is indeed that which is presupposed by the diversification of the sects."[37]

One could agree unreservedly with Küng's observations if in the course of history the particular sects had in fact emerged in response to some doctrine contained in the canon. But what is the situation when the appeal to a given theological position supported by certain canonical writings of the New Testament constitutes only a minor factor in the dissolution of the Church's unity? Or if the appeal to the canon represents only a *retrospective* justification of a breach which has already taken place, and the background to which is to be found more in the sphere of political and intellectual changes than in the New Testament? Or when — to mention only a third possibility — it turns out that only one single division of the Church can be justified by invoking some part of the canonical writings?

H. Küng feels the position he has adopted against E. Käsemann to be unsatisfactory, and therefore continues: "But given the disunity of the canon as a presupposition, how does the multiplicity of the sects arise from this? This question is not to be answered merely by pointing to the disunity of the canon, because for all its disunity the canon of the New Testament is still *one*, and is publicly accepted as *one* by the Church — in the course of a history subject to what are certainly exceptional vicissitudes. This shows that the different witnesses were understood not negatively as offering some store of doctrine as a 'rival programme' to the gospel, but positively as the appropriate expression of that gospel, and as deriving from it. This, then, is the question: How is it that a multiplicity of sects has grown up, when the canon of the New Testament, for all its internal disunity, is

[37] *Ibid.,* pp. 401 ff.

106

nevertheless *one*"[38] Küng's answer is: "by *choice*. In other words, because men have not accepted deeply enough the canon of the New Testament, *one* in spite of all its internal disunity, and because they have not striven hard enough to gain an understanding *of the whole* — in spite of all the difficulties that lie in their path. It is because instead of this men exploit the disunity of the one canon in order to arrive at a choice from among its contents, even though it is one canon. By this means man can achieve, under certain circumstances, an impressive concentration of the *kerygma*; but at the same time he diminishes that *kerygma*, and he does this at the expense of the New Testament and of the unity of the Church which stands behind that canon."[39] In this refusal to accept the whole Küng sees "an understanding of Scripture which favours *hairesis*",[40] and he continues: "Thus upon an accurate view of the matter one is compelled to say: In its disunity the New Testament canon is indeed a *presupposition*, an *occasion* of the multiplicity of sects, but not, in the strict sense, the *cause* or *origin* of this. The combustible material, the house timber contained in a house, can indeed be the presupposed condition, the occasion of its being set on fire; but the cause and origin of the fire is the incendiary who sets fire to the wood. The true cause (in the strict sense) of the multiplicity of the sects is not the New Testament canon, which, considered in its unity as 'catholic' (καθ' ὅλου) is the presupposed condition of the unity of the ἐκκλησία, but αἵρεσις, which dissolves the unity of the ἐκκλησία."[41]

Now if we take the New Testament itself as our criterion, then both these theories, Käsemann's and Küng's respectively, appear untenable in principle. Käsemann holds that the canon is the *cause* of the multiplicity of the sects; Küng would regard it as a *presupposed condition,* an *occasion* of this multiplicity. But in the New Testament the idea of heresy ever arising as a result of

---

[38] *Ibid.,* p. 402. [39] *Ibid.*
[40] *Ibid.,* p. 403. [41] *Ibid.*

men's selecting particular writings within the canon is quite unknown.[42] According to Galatians 5:20 heresy, division (one group of men, one school separating themselves from the rest) arises from the fact that men within the community of the Church do "the works of the flesh". The heresies that arise from this, therefore, consist in "the forming of groups or cliques within the community which are radically and diametrically opposed to the unity of the Church as the open and just assembly of the people of God".[43] In 1 Corinthians 11:19 Paul goes a step further when he says: "There must be αἱρέσεις (factions) among you in order that those who are genuine among you may be recognized." According to Titus 3:10 intercourse with the αἱρετικὸς ἄνθρωπος (haereticus homo, heretic) must be broken off. Another passage states: "But false prophets also arose among the people, just as there will be false teachers among you, who will secretly bring in destructive heresies (αἱρέσεις ἀπωλείας), even denying the Master who bought them, bringing upon themselves swift destruction. And many will follow their licentiousness, and because of them the way of truth will be reviled. And in their greed they will exploit you with false words. From of old their condemnation has not been idle, and their destruction has not been asleep" (2 Pet 2:1–3). Here too heresy, in the sense intended in Galatians 5:20, is traced back to its origin in wickedness, evil intent and the "works of the flesh".[44] There is no question of any kind of selection of writings from the canon, however, made. Thus the

---

[42] On αἵρεσις see H. Schlier in *TWNT*, vol. I, pp. 180 ff.; H. E. Turner, *The Pattern of Christian Truth. A Study in the Relations between Orthodoxy and Heresy in the Early Church* (1964); L. Goppelt, "Kirche und Häresie nach Paulus", *Gedenkschrift für D. W. Elert* (1955), pp. 9–23; M. Meinertz, "Σχίσμα und αἵρεσις im Neuen Testament", *TZ* 1 (1957), pp. 114–18. See further S. L. Greenslade, "Der Begriff der Häresie in der alten Kirche" in K. E. Skydsgaard and L. Vischer, eds., *Schrift und Tradition* (1963), pp. 24–44.

[43] H. Schlier, *Der Brief an die Galater* (12th ed., 1962), p. 254.

[44] On the special nature of the struggle against the heretics in 2 Peter see K. H. Schelkle, *Die Petrusbriefe — der Judasbrief* (1961), pp. 230–4.

attempts to connect the question of the canon with heresy and the diversity of sects can be rejected.[45]

But what has been said so far still leaves the question raised by Käsemann unanswered. If it is taken as axiomatic that the causes of the Reformation can really be traced back to specific assertions in the canonical books, then it must be conceded as a fact that in this unique case the canon has not, of itself, been able to ensure the preservation of the Church's unity — indeed that it actually seems to justify a cleavage. In the present state of this cleavage the canon plays an important part. Käsemann perceives this with a sure eye. The only question is in what sense do the words of the apostle concerning the necessity of divisions "in order that those who are genuine among you may be recognized" (1 Cor 11:19) apply to this particular division? Taking as our basis that the canon is a collection of sacred writings which are binding upon the covenant people, we may say a few words on this point.[46] By the formation of the canon the Church has rejected the writings which she considers alien, and has thereby enabled men to recognize which writings she regards as binding upon her members in this world. This means that the Church as a whole has a duty to fulfil with regard to the canon as a whole: she must conduct her life according to what is said in these books. With the formation of the canon a probable danger is averted, that namely of *gnosis*; but the canon itself, now established once and for all, contains a new element of danger within itself, namely that of the selection of particular writings, the possibility of so restricting one's position that one accepts only a section of the canonical books.

Now the question which demands an answer in the concrete is this: at what point in the Church's history up to the present

---

[45] *Ibid.,* p. 234.
[46] In his "Häretiker im Urchristentum als theologisches Problem", *Zeit und Geschichte. Dankesgabe an R. Bultmann zum 80. Geburtstag* (1964), pp. 61–76, H. Koester attempts a theological evaluation of heresy which raises noteworthy questions.

has a cleavage taken place (such as, for instance, that of the Reformation) which has claimed to be supported by the authority of the canon?[47] The answer to this question must be that when men confine themselves to a particular section of the canonical writings and appeal to them as their authority, this procedure represents a reaction made necessary by the fact that in their practical lives these men have already formed themselves into a special faction within the Church; their separation from the rest is already an accomplished fact. This in turn amounts to raising a further question: in what sense are we to understand the statement that there must be divisions in order that the Church can be proved? Is the sense in which we are to take this as follows? — In certain cases a group of men, reacting, as we have seen, to a situation in which they are already placed, appeals to a particular section of the canonical writings to justify their position. When this happens, it should have the effect of bringing the Church itself back to a state in which it orders its practical life according to the canonical writings as a whole. The question which we have put above must be answered in the affirmative; this is indeed the sense in which the saying referred to should be taken.

Thus when E. Käsemann so restricts himself that he will recognize as canonically binding only that element in the canon which is the doctrine of justification, he acknowledges that what he has given his allegiance to is only one point in the canon, albeit a central one. Moreover the group associated with him in being cut off from the main body of the Church appealing for its justification to this same element in the gospel, represents a reaction against a Church which, in her practical life, has allowed this point to be neglected. Since the people of God has the duty of maintaining the covenant in its entirety, it is of little use to point out that the doctrine which is invoked to justify the cleavage

[47] Luther raises the question of the canon in his dispute with Eck at Leipzig in 1519.

is also to be found in the Church's books, or even that it has at least always been represented there in some form or other. Thus what we have said must be considered to apply to this division too: that its function is to recall the *whole* of the canonical writings to the Church's mind, to remind her of what she has to carry out in her concrete life.

While the effect of division upon the Church, accepting, as she does, the canon in its entirety, is to urge her to accord to the canonical writings rather more than mere lip-service, the division which has taken place succumbs to the danger of turning a position which was necessary in a particular set of circumstances into a permanent and rigid system applicable in all circumstances. This applies even to the doctrine of justification. For since the problem of the justice of God and the justification of the sinner is a Semitic one[48] it must necessarily have been pushed into the background among the communities of Gentile Christians. The experience which these men received of Christianity was affected by their different tradition, and took place in a different way from the experience of Paul, the disciple of Jewish teachers. The Hellenistic community was something new.[49] Thus while the course of the Church, continuing unbroken down the ages, was subject to, and in certain milieux even demanded changes,[50] still we must not allow this fact to make us forget those historical events which constitute the prior condition of the Church's course considered as a whole. The fact that the Church is tied to historical events necessarily demands that the justification of the

[48] W. von Soden in *RGG* 5 (1961), col. 1693; cf. E. Käsemann, "Gottesgerechtigkeit bei Paulus", *ZTK* 58 (1961), pp. 370 f., on the Old Testament background of the doctrine of the justice of God in Paul.
[49] See E. Käsemann, "Paulus und der Frühkatholizismus", *ZTK* 60 (1963), pp. 82 ff., cf. also H. Conzelmann, "Heidenchristentum", *RGG* 3 (1959), cols. 129 ff.
[50] K. H. Schelkle, *Die Petrusbriefe — Der Judasbrief,* p. 245, rightly emphasizes that it is not possible to confine the message of the New Testament to a particular moment.

sinner by the righteousness of God shall at all times be maintained and borne in mind as a truth of prime importance.

Even in this case of justification, however, what we have said still applies. It is necessary to bear in mind that to petrify this doctrine in a rigid system is to falsify it, and to lead men astray from the true path. Thus as a result of changes in the course of history the question of justification as it arises today is different from what it was at the time of the Reformation.[51] It maintains its position of central importance, but is viewed in an altered perspective. In the Church's past the canon has fulfilled various functions, according as, in the particular circumstances of any given period, it has been felt necessary to put into effect in the Church's life the truth of sacred Scripture as set down in the canon. It would hardly be an admissible procedure, therefore, to interpret a single historical situation as a permanent prototype to which all others must conform.[52]

---

[51] P. Schütz, *Parusia* (1963), pp. 93 ff. gives a penetrating assessment of the present situation, in which justifying faith is no longer understood, as it was at the beginning of the Reformation, as the ultimate essence of the revealed truth of the Bible: "Now it is the same faith which is understood as an *epistemological principle* for historical criticism. This is what happens in so-called de-mythologizing" (*ibid.,* p. 93). From this point of view we can also understand why justification cannot constitute a major point in the current discussion of how the Churches are to be re-united. Insofar as Protestants and Catholics have come closer to each other's positions on this point, the signs of this coming together are by and large the explanations which have been given of so-called 'misunderstandings'. On this see above all the discussion with Karl Barth in H. Küng's *Rechtfertigung. Die Lehre Karl Barths und eine katholische Besinnung* (1957), E. T.: *Justification. The Doctrine of Karl Barth and a Catholic Reflection* (1965); G. Gloege, "Die Rechtfertigungslehre als hermeneutische Kategorie", *TLZ* 89 (1964), cols. 161–76, attempts to elucidate the question of how, in spite of the difficulties experienced today, the doctrine of justification may be considered the key to Scripture.

[52] In my opinion the attempt of E. Haible, "Der Kanon des Neuen Testamentes als Modellfall einer kirchlichen Wiedervereinigung", *TrTZ* 78 (1966), pp. 11–27, or that of E. Käsemann, exhibit a tendency to excessive historical generalization.

The ultimate question, however, is always whether the Church's life is in conformity with the truth contained in the biblical writings. Now the final answer to this question is to be found neither by scientific research nor by arbitrary reliance on so-called scriptural texts but by obedience to the Spirit of truth who leads the Church through the ages with all their diversity.[53]

Vatican II, continuing the previous teaching of the Church in *Dei Verbum,* also connects the question of canonicity directly with that of the inspiration of Scripture by the Holy Spirit (ch. III, art. 11). The canonical books constitute the guiding principle of the Christian life for they are all without restriction of any kind, the work of the Holy Spirit and teach the truth of salvation (ch. III, art. 11).

[53] Views on the operation of the Holy Spirit have a most profound influence on, for instance, the statements of the reformers concerning the question of canonicity. Cf., e.g., Appel, *Kanon,* pp. 28 ff.

CHAPTER SEVEN

SCRIPTURE'S CLAIM TO BE REVEALED AS ABSOLUTE TRUTH

In the course of time the frontiers have shifted, and it has become progressively clearer where a stand must be made once and for all for the truth, and which elements in Scripture may be conceded to have only a temporal application. Even when the realization (which is already to be found in Augustine) had become established that Scripture does not teach truths of natural science and that its claim to veracity does not apply to statements made in this field, there still remained the further troublesome question of inerrancy in respect of historical statements.

Whether the Bible itself is historically true, and whether the deeds of divine salvation recorded in it really took place — for the believer these questions are crucial. His answer to them is in the affirmative, and this answer still holds good even if, to take one example, it can be shown that not all the numbers recorded in Scripture turn out to be historically accurate. There is no reason on this account to accuse Scripture of lying. For Scripture's claim to veracity differs from that of modern science precisely on this point. The concept of truth which is regarded as axiomatic for modern history writing is the "idea of verifiable factuality" or "what the evidence obliges us to believe" (Collingwood).[1]

---

[1] J. Moltmann, "Exegese und Eschatologie der Geschichte", *EvTh* 22 (1962), p. 37.

What Scripture understands by 'truth', on the other hand, is above all faithfulness and steadfastness.

It is this biblical concept of truth that the Church is speaking of when she declares that Scripture is completely and absolutely without error.

Even in view of the conclusions of the natural and historical sciences, then, the Church is fully justified in speaking of Scripture as inerrant. Nevertheless we cannot omit to say also that the Bible's claim to veracity is often understood in a false sense, because in asserting this claim for Scripture a concept of truth is often invoked which is foreign to Scripture itself. The difficulty of finding a realistic solution to the problem of truth in the Bible has been aggravated by the fact that some, who certainly perceived the new difficulties and intended to solve them, have, nevertheless, persisted in adhering to concepts of truth which belong to scholastic or still more Cartesian metaphysics, but which are alien to the Bible. Attempts to tackle the problem along these lines have been unable to offer any convincing solutions to it.

The Bible's claim to veracity implies that with reference to the making of the covenant God has revealed himself in the history subsequent to this, that he has remained faithful to his words and promises, and also that he will be true to them in the future. This being the case, then, it will be useful to determine the nature of this claim still more precisely with reference to other religions. In what sense does Scripture, and thereby Christianity too claim to be true?

Christianity's claim to absolute truth is 'absolute' in two ways: on the one hand it admits of no exception to this truth which God has embodied in Scripture — for otherwise God himself would stand condemned as a liar;[2] on the other hand this claim is unique,

---

[2] G. Rosenkranz points out that today Christianity's claim to absolute truth is defensible only in the sense of ἀλήθεια as it appears in the Johannine Gospel. One point against Rosenkranz that must be mentioned is that the Johannine usage, as compared with the rest of Scripture, is peripheral; cf. above, pp. 85 f., nn. 33–35. In a broad attempt to find fresh ground for Christianity's claim to

for no other people has ever made a covenant with the unique God,[3] or, indeed has a covenant ever been made between a god and a specific people.

Now that contact with other religions and with heathens has been made possible for every Christian of the present day, we are, in effect, confronted with a demand to which it is impossible to turn a deaf ear,[4] namely that the absolute truth which is claimed for revelation and Scripture shall be understood in a sense which conforms to the biblical concept of truth. The course of events has brought us to a point at which it is no longer possible to maintain a false interpretation of Christianity's claim to absolute veracity.[5] Neither in the sphere of international relations nor

absolute truth W. Philipp, *Die Absolutheit des Christentums und die Summe der Anthropologie* (1959), has made some highly original suggestions which, however, have only slight basis in Scripture. On the discussion of Christianity's claim to absolute truth up to the present cf. A. Lang, *Fundamentaltheologie,* vol. II (3rd ed., 1962), pp. 216 ff. On the problems regarding Christianity's place among the world religions cf. J. Ratzinger, "Der christliche Glaube und die Weltreligionen", *Gott in Welt — Festgabe für K. Rahner,* vol. II (1964), pp. 287–305.

[3] Scripture's claims to veracity and to authority in an absolute sense cannot therefore be shaken by evidence of the existence of pure monotheism among some other people, e. g. the monotheism of Zarathustra. Cf. R. Mayer, "Monotheismus in Israel und in der Religion Zarathustras", *BZ* 1 (1957), pp. 23–58.

[4] J. Hessen's *Der Absolutheitsanspruch des Christentums* (1963), is intended to further this aim from the standpoint of the philosophy of religion.

[5] What place Hegel assumes in the history of the attempts to substantiate Christianity's claim to absolute truth is a matter of dispute. K. Lowith, "Hegels Aufhebung der christlichen Religion", *Ansichten — Festschrift G. Krüger* (1962), pp. 156–203, is of the opinion that Hegel's attempt to substantiate this claim on philosophical grounds ultimately turns into the most decisive attack against this claim. By his identification of absolute truth with absolute spirit he distorts Christian teaching. This interpretation of Hegel's is contradicted with the utmost sharpness by C. G. Schweitzer, *Neue Zeitschrift für systematische Theologie und Religionsphilosophie* 5 (1963), pp. 248–62. On Hegel's definition of the "absolute truth" of the Christian religion see his *Vorlesungen über die Philosophie der Religion,* Jubilee Edition, vol. XVI, pp. 207 f. In his article, "Nietzsches Idee der Wahrheit und die Wahrheit der Philosophie",

in that of domestic politics can Christians occupy themselves with maintaining a claim to absolute truth according to the old label — as, for example, by claiming that the Bible evinces a higher level of culture than the literature of other peoples. This would not merely be ineffectual in practice; it would also be untenable in the Church's own eyes.

When an attempt to justify Christianity's claim to absolute veracity unfortunately collapses for want of a sound basis, then one may, from sheer weariness, evade the main issue in this vexatious question and turn instead to the problem of tolerance. But such a procedure often amounts to no more than a rear-guard action that is forced upon us.

Again, while unsuitable arguments are often advanced in the attempt to justify this claim to absolute veracity, still to suppose that this claim must finally be abandoned would amount to a misconception of the reality involved. The witness of Scripture is opposed to this. A Christian faith that is based upon the Scriptures accepts that God is absolutely faithful or 'true' to his people, and all God's words have been fulfilled in truth in his Son (cf. 2 Cor 1:19 ff.). This 'true-ness' of God in his Son is absolute, neither able to be revoked nor capable of being perfected further (Heb 1:1). Only by denying its own nature can Christianity surrender this claim to absolute truth.

Scripture, then, claims to be true in a special sense, and its claim is based upon the fact that it records God's revelation of

Philosophisches Jahrbuch 70 (1962/63), p. 309, K. Ulmer writes: "The uncompromising demand that philosophical knowledge must be absolute knowledge derives from the philosophy of the modern age. It represents a reaction against the 'absolute revelation' claimed for Christianity, its diametrical opposite. In this respect philosophy betrays an unjustifiable dependence upon Christian theology. This dependence is also apparent in Nietzsche. The idea of the eternal return can be shown to be the outcome of an extreme reaction against the idea of an absolute God with reference to his power over history." In holding this view Ulmer must also see that the 'unjustifiable dependence (of philosophy) upon Christian theology' presupposes in its turn the dependence of theology upon philosophy.

himself at the making of the covenant. Now if this true, then it also brings the correct light to bear upon the attempts which have been made to explain the uniqueness of the Bible (and with this its claim to be utterly and unreservedly true) as the outcome of a peculiar quality inherent in the Bible itself and deriving from the language or literary forms in which it is written. All efforts of this kind are doomed to failure. The reason is not far to seek. Since, for example, the Scriptures are written in human language, that which is peculiar to the Scriptures cannot be inherent in their language, but rather in what they actually say. Hence those who set out to ascribe the unique quality of the Bible in any way to the language in which it is expressed are doomed to disappointment. For they only succeed in throwing light upon the historical origins of the language, and thereby show precisely that it cannot of itself be derived from revelation.

Those who attempt to explain the special place of the Bible from its language or from some special quality of Hebrew thought arouse the suspicion that their theories are at basis simply a remnant left over from the time when Hebrew was regarded as the original language of humanity.[6] Such theories overlook the fact that it was by her history with God as the people of the covenant[7] that Israel was separated from the world about her, and not by a particular mode of thought or a special kind of language; it is not in this manner that thought and language are to be connected.

Since in making the covenant God accepted the speech of the

---

[6] Cf. p. 153, n. 32.

[7] On the significance of the concept, 'people' for the history of Israel see W. von Soden, *BiOr* 16 (1959), p. 131; A. Cody, "When is the Chosen People Called a Gôy?", *VT* 14 (1964), pp. 1–6. On the significance of the 'people of God' idea for the Old and New Testaments, with a bibliography of the relevant literature see F. Mussner, "'Volk Gottes' im Neuen Testament", *TrTZ* 72 (1963), pp. 169–78. This idea attracted considerable notice at Vatican II, cf. A. Grillmeier's commentary on *Lumen Gentium,* ch. ii, in H. Vorgrimler, ed., *Commentary on the Documents of Vatican II*, vol. I (1967), pp. 153 ff.

Israelites as the language of his pact with them, it was in human language that he imparted knowledge of himself to them. In this manner he laid under contribution human language with all its possibilities as an instrument for imparting revelation. It is the investigation of literary *genres* that, more than any other factor, has shown this to be the case.

Knowledge of God himself has been given by the self-revelation of God in word and deed, the words and deeds of his Son included. He who thus reveals himself is not yet definitively shown forth. Word and deed alike are wanting in final clarity, so that the deed has need of the word that points its significance, while the word has need of the fulfilling deed in which its veracity is attested. For this reason Scripture speaks of word and deed in the same way, and does not present the one as dialectically opposed to the other.

But even in Israel, where God reveals himself by word and deed, it still remains an enduring fact that "truly thou art God, who hidest thyself, O God of Israel, the Saviour!" (Is 45:15.)[8]

Revelation, therefore, always entails a certain hiddenness. This is also shown by the fact that it is not all men who can recognize it. In this way the hiddenness of revelation prevents the revelation of God in history from being inescapably evident. Only he upon whom God bestows the grace of faith perceives

---

[8] With reference to the relevant passages P. Althaus, "Offenbarung als Geschichte und Glaube", *TLZ* 87 (1962), cols. 321–30, shows that Pannenberg's thesis to the effect that revelation in history is open to him who has eyes to see is devoid of scriptural basis. L. Steiger too, "Offenbarungsgeschichte und theologische Vernunft. Zur Theologie W. Pannenberg", *ZTK* 59 (1962), pp. 108 f., and H. Gollwitzer, *Die Existenz Gottes im Bekenntnis des Glaubens* (2nd ed., 1963), pp. 114–17, advance ideas of a similar kind against Pannenberg's thesis. On the 'veiled' character of revelation see further W. Bulst, *Offenbarung* (1960), pp. 101–4; G. von Rad, *Theologie des Alten Testaments,* vol. II (3rd ed., 1962), pp. 387 ff., E. T.: *Theology of the Old Testament,* vol. II (1966); W. Pannenberg has replied to the criticisms of P. Althaus ("Offenbarung als Geschichte und Glaube", cols. 81–92), but his answer is unsatisfactory in certain respects. See G. Muschalek, *ZKT* 86 (1964), pp. 191 ff.

that God has revealed himself here. On this quality of hiddenness in revelation, and on its overall effects upon the life of faith, P. Althaus percipiently remarks: "The hiddenness of revelation implies a *testing*. Faith as the recognition of revelation continues to be kept alive, but only by *overcoming* the constant temptation of the *'incognito'*, the 'weakness of God' in his revelation. It is not only faith as trust in *salvation* that lives, but also, and prior to this, faith as sureness concerning God's revelation in the history of Jesus. The believer knows of this temptation from his own experience. Therefore he also has an understanding of those who do not overcome the temptation to which the hiddenness gives rise. He knows that the possibility of unbelief is inherent in the very manner in which God bestows revelation. Hence he can no longer conceive of unbelief in purely human terms as a sinful blindness. The sin of shutting out God, and with him the reality of his revelation in history — this is something that he too knows indeed, and from his own experience. In this respect he is no different from the unbeliever. For this reason he experiences his ability to believe as a grace, a miracle; and he can trace the riddle that next to faith here stands unbelief there back to its source not in the sinfulness of our hearts but in the mystery of the free election of God, who gives here and denies there. This is altered neither by the fact that the revelation in history is directed to all men, nor by the oecumenical duty laid upon Christendom of preaching the gospel to all."[9]

[9] P. Althaus, "Offenbarung als Geschichte und Glaube", col. 328. It is not possible, within the limits imposed here, to enter into the question of how far the Church is 'visible' or 'invisible'. On the discussion of this problem cf. E. Kinder, "Die Verborgenheit der Kirche nach Luther", *Festgabe Josef Lortz* I (1958), pp. 173–92; H. Bacht, "Die Sichtbarkeit der Kirche im kontrovers-theologischen Gespräch der Gegenwart", *Einsicht und Glaube — Festschrift G. Söhngen* (1962), pp. 447–63; M. Honecker, *Kirche als Gestalt und Ereignis. Die sichtbare Gestalt der Kirchen als dogmatisches Problem* (1963). J. L. Witte, "Zu den vier Wesenszügen der Kirche", *Gott in Welt — Festgabe für K. Rahner*, vol. II, p. 441, n. 30, brings out the point that according to Catholic teaching even in her character as visible the Church of Christ is a mystery to be believed,

A characteristic that arises from the peculiar nature of biblical revelation and its claim to veracity is the place given to 'remembering'[10] within the Bible,[11] and, as a consequence, in the lives of those who accept the canon of the Scriptures. Whereas in Greek the importance accorded to remembering was influenced by linguistic considerations,[12] in the Bible the significance of remembering is based upon history.

although visible signs may be apparent in the Church of Christ even to unbelievers. On the teaching of Vatican II concerning the visibility of the Church see A. Grillmeier's commentary on *Lumen Gentium,* art. 8, in *Commentary on the Documents of Vatican II,* vol. I, pp. 146 ff.

[10] 'Remembering, remembrance, memory' is in many respects of fundamental importance for men whose life is circumscribed by temporal conditions. Hence the central position which these ideas assume in the Old and New Testaments is to a large extent based upon human nature itself. With reference to the various aspects (physiological, philosophical etc.) cf. A. Seifert, "Die Struktur der Erinnerung", *Philosophia naturalis,* vol. I (1950), pp. 415–34, 511–31; *ibid.,* vol. II (1952), pp. 50–71; P. Lersch, *Aufbau der Person* (7th ed., 1956), pp. 28 f., 353–69; W. Porzig, *Das Wunder der Sprache* (1962), pp. 169 ff.; H. Vogel, "Memoria — Historia. Eine Frage, angeregt durch Augustin", *EvTh* 23 (1963), pp. 393–404.

[11] On the question of 'remembering' in the Old Testament cf. H. Gross, "Zur Wurzel *zkr*", *BZ* 4 (1960), pp. 227–37; T. A. H. de Boer, *Gedanken und Gedächtnis in der Welt des Alten Testaments* (1962); O. Haggenmüller, "Erinnern und Vergessen Gottes und der Menschen", *Bibel und Leben* 3 (1962), pp. 1–15, 79–89, 193–202; B. S. Childs, *Memory and Tradition in Israel* (1962), and W. Schottroff, *'Gedenken' im Alten Orient und im Alten Testament* (1964), give comprehensive treatments of the question of memory in the Old Testament. On 'remembering' in the New Testament cf. N. A. Dahl, "Anamnesis. Mémoire et Commémoration dans le christianisme primitif", *Studia Theologica* 1 (1947), pp. 69–95; N. Füglister, *Die Heilsbedeutung des Pascha* (1963), p. 288; H. Schlier, "Zum Begriff des Geistes nach dem Johannesevangelium", *Neutestamentliche Aufsätze — Festschrift J. Schmid* (1963), p. 235.

[12] E. Heitsch, "Die nicht-philosophische ΑΛΗΘΕΙΑ", *Hermes* 90 (1962), p. 33, n. 1, makes the point that "... for Plato the connection between remembering (= not forgetting) and truth (= unconcealment) ... was inherent in the very etymology of ἀ-λήθεια." In Heitsch's article the previous discussion concerning the Greek concept of truth is summed up, and he writes in conclusion: "If it has been shown that at all periods — and of course the ...

Some of the salvific deeds of God are to be remembered as the motivations for the making of the covenant,[13] while others, those deeds which God performed after the covenant had been broken, attest the fact of his faithfulness (truth) to the covenant, which is still in force. In order to recall the making of the covenant the original proclamation had to be read again at stated intervals. In this way men were prevented from forgetting the covenant.[14]

The act of 'remembering' retains this special importance in the new covenant. At the time when this is instituted Christ lays it as a duty upon those who belong to the new covenant people that they shall think of him.[15]

In this respect too the old and new covenants have replaced the 'mythology of remembering and forgetting'[16] by that kind

---

later witnesses too must be accorded their due importance here — it was natural for the Greeks to think of ἀ-λήθεια, we have to be clear upon the exact meaning of this word ... A decisive factor is that ἀλήθεια, as applied to an object, has the force of 'without concealment', but as applied to a statement has the force of 'truth'; ἀλήθεια is primarily a quality of the world, considered as constituting the essential objectivity of things; the German word for truth, on the other hand, signifies a quality of judgments that are passed concerning those objective things ... A further consequence arising out of this, and relevant to the point that linguistic usage here has been determined by etymology, is that the quality of ἀληθής is only secondarily applied to assertions or statements; thus Homeric usages such as εἰπεῖν etc. originally meant not 'to speak the truth, so to express something that it is true, i.e. corresponds to the reality', but 'to express that which is unconcealed, open to view' (or, for the sake of greater clarity, 'something which already appears in the world to be unconcealed is then put into words')." Ibid., pp. 31 f.

[13] Cf. BF, pp. 21, 29 f., 48.

[14] Ibid., pp. 28, 68–70.

[15] H. Kosmala, "'Das tut zu meinem Gedächtnis'", NT 4 (1960), pp. 81–94. T. Neuenzeit, Das Herrenmahl (1960), pp. 111–15, 133–46. It is an assured conclusion that the New Testament command to 'remember' can only be understood from the background of the Old Testament and the covenant idea. Cf. Neuenzeit, ibid., pp. 143 ff.

[16] M. Eliade, "Die Mythologie des Erinnerns und des Vergessens", Antaios 5 (1963), pp. 28–47; id., "Mythologies of Memory and Forgetting", History of Religions, vol. II (1962/63), pp. 329–44, treats of this question from the

of remembering that is based on history[17] and on persons, a remembrance of the faithfulness which has been promised. This kind of remembering makes it possible to attain to hope[18] in God and life with him.

In the language of the Bible 'remembering' is directly connected with the name. For by his deeds, in which his faithfulness is revealed, God has made for himself that name which alone endures, and which will be remembered for ever. Every other name will be forgotten.[19] Then in the New Testament we are told that the name of Jesus is the sole means by which salvation is imparted to mankind. Thus the essential point in the Bible's claim to veracity might be formulated as: "Only in the name of Jesus will salvation be imparted to mankind" (Acts 4:12).

A further aspect of Scripture's claim to veracity is interior to the Bible, and affects the linguistic relationship between the Old Testament and the New. Since the New Testament is presented as the fulfilment of the Old it must show that in Christ God has kept faith with Israel. Now since the evidence for this can only be presented through the medium of human language, it gives rise to the question of the truth of the literary presentation of this history, i.e. we are confronted with the question of the use of Old Testament passages in the New. The theory of the *sensus plenior* is partly aimed at finding a solution to this problem.[20]

standpoint of the science of religions in general, and in the course of his treatment incidentally draws attention to the special position of the Israelites.
[17] With reference to the anthropological meaning of the promise, J. Moltmann refers, in his article, "Exegese und Eschatologie der Geschichte", p. 47, n. 36, to O. F. Bollnow, *Wesen und Wandel der Tugenden* (1958), pp. 168 ff.
[18] On the relationship between hope and remembering see J. Moltmann, "Exegese und Eschatologie", pp. 62 ff.
[19] On the problem of the connections between 'name', 'remembering' and 'forgetting' cf. n. 10.
[20] On the history of the *sensus plenior* and the present state of the discussion concerning it cf. R. A. Brown, *The Sensus Plenior of Sacred Scripture* (1955); id., "The Sensus Plenior in the Last Ten Years", *CBQ* 25 (1963), pp. 262–85; B. Vawter, "The Fuller Sense: Some Considerations", *CBQ* 26 (1964),

God who spoke in the old covenant has acted in the new in accordance with the word which he then uttered.[21] The New Testament presents the events caused by him as prefigured and predicted in the Old, and attempts to prove the connection between them by referring to specific passages. This being the case, the problem inevitably arises to what extent do the passages concerned in the Old Testament foretell the New Testament which is to come? But since it could not be proved from the actual text of the Old Testament passages that according to the rules of modern philology they did have this connection with the New, the investigators, in order to solve this problem, have had recourse to the *sensus plenior* (also called the 'fuller' or 'deeper' sense). This cannot be something retrospectively 'read into' a scriptural passage; it must rather be something "intended from the outset by the Holy Spirit who inspires" even "in cases in which it remained concealed from the biblical author, and perhaps from many of the generations which came after him".[22]

Our estimate of the *sensus plenior* theory must take account of the fact that it represents an attempt to explain the claims to veracity of the Old Testament as compared with the New in the light of modern difficulties. This theory could only have been formulated after it had been realized that the New Testament interpretation of Old Testament passages is not absolute but subject to the conditions prevailing at a particular epoch. What the exponents of the *sensus plenior* were seeking to achieve was to establish the 'truth' of the New Testament mode of interpretation by broadening the sense of the Old Testament passages so as to allow for it. At basis, then, does this not represent a tendency

---

pp. 85–96. Vawter adopts a critical position with regard to the *sensus plenior* theory.

[21] Cf. J. Michl, "Dogmatischer Schriftbeweis und Exegese", *BZ* 2 (1958), p. 8.

[22] *Ibid.* The upholders of the *sensus plenior* theory do not give a clear picture of how the concept is to be more precisely defined. Cf. Brown, "Sensus Plenior in the Last Ten Years", pp. 263 ff. They are, however, all united upon the point that the 'full sense' was originally a hidden sense.

towards artificial harmonization after a pattern which we can already discern in Augustine's efforts to solve the problems of interpretation?[23]

On the question of how Old and New Testament passages are related we must notice first that an unbroken line of history can be traced leading from the old covenant to the new one. The covenant idea lived on in the New Testament; at the same time the language of the Old Testament, shaped as it was by tradition, worked its way in to the New Testament.[24] In view of these two factors also, then, a considerable agreement between the two collections of texts is to be expected, but must we go further and subscribe to the view that the reason for this agreement is the alleged presence in the Old Testament of a *sensus plenior,* which can only be discerned in the light of the events recorded in the New Testament? In solving this question we must take as our starting-point the question of how the New Testament authors themselves regarded this connection between their writings and those of the Old.

If we want to see this question in its true light, to estimate how significant the use of the Old Testament in the New really is, and what is the true connection between the Old Testament and the events recorded in the New, then we must take due cognizance of a factor which, though generally recognized and accepted, is too often merely mentioned in passing. This is that the New Testament authors view the Old Testament from their own standpoint.[25] To apply this in the concrete, then, we need an approach which will enable us to view the Old Testament passages in the perspective of the 'event' of Christ, and in the light of sub-

---

[23] Cf. B. Vawter, "The Fuller Sense", p. 90.
[24] Cf., e.g., K. Beyer, *Semitische Syntax im Neuen Testament,* vol. I, part 1 (1962), pp. 7–11.
[25] Cf. J. Michl, "Dogmatischer Schriftbeweis und Exegese", p. 10: "Primitive Christianity interprets the Old Testament in the light of the 'event' of Christ"; J. Schmid, "Die alttestamentlichen Zitate bei Paulus und die Theorie vom sensus plenior", *BZ* 3 (1959), p. 162.

sequent history, and we shall find this approach in the methods of explaining Scripture which prevailed at the time in question. It is possible to recapture in all essentials what this method of explaining and interpreting Scripture was. The New Testament authors interpreted the Old Testament according to the methods which were in force in the Judaism of the period.[26]

[26] J. Schmid, *ibid.,* remarks that despite the different starting-points adopted by Paul and the rabbis, "one cannot see any difference in *method* between Paul on the one hand and the rabbis and scribes of Qumran on the other", and that, conversely, one is justified in saying "that when Paul gives a Christological interpretation to the Old Testament he is making it applicable to the present in precisely the same way as the author of the Qumran Habakkuk commentary made it applicable to his period and circumstances". Cf. also K. H. Schelkle, "Hermeneutische Zeugnisse im Neuen Testament", *BZ* 6 (1962), pp. 161 ff.; W. G. Kümmel, "Schriftauslegung im Urchristentum", *RGG* V (1961), cols. 1517 ff.; J. A. Fitzmyer, "The Use of Explicit Old Testament Quotations in Qumran Literature and in the New Testament", *NTS* 7 (1960/61), p. 330, arrives as a result of his researches at the following conclusion: "We may characterize both the Qumran and the New Testament use of the Old Testament *in general* as a literal exegesis, when this is defined in opposition to the allegorical exegesis of Philo and the Alexandrian school of later times. There are, it is true, some allegorical interpretations in both, but these are not characteristic. Nor is it a *strictly literal* exegesis which respects the original meaning and context of the words quoted; however, examples of this do occur occasionally. Normally it was an exegesis based on the words quoted, even though the relevance of them to their historical setting meant very little to the Qumran or New Testament writers ... Again, common to both was the explicit desire to enhance some recent event in their histories or some idea or person with an Old Testament association, as a result of a certain analogy which they saw between the event and some event in Israel's history." On the midrashic and haggadic methods of interpretation as employed by the New Testament authors cf. also J. A. Fitzmyer, " 'Now this Melchizedek . . .' (Heb 7:1)", *CBQ* 25 (1963), pp. 205–31; J. Coppens, "Les arguments scripturaires et leur portée dans les lettres pauliniennes", *Studiorum Paulinorum Congressus Internationalis Catholicus, 1961,* vol. II (1963), pp. 243–53; R. T. Mead, "A Dissenting Opinion about Respect for Context in Old Testament Quotations", *NTS* 10 (1964), pp. 279–89; A. G. Wright, "The Literary Genre Midrash", *CBQ* 28 (1966), pp. 105–38. This author now provides a comprehensive account of the character of midrashic literature.

They differ from other Jewish interpreters not in the methods they use, but only in the matter of their interpretation — although this difference is, of course, a radical one.[27] Apart from cases in which an Old Testament passage is cited in its original sense,[28] the Old Testament is interpreted from a position which has already been taken up, with the result that it is not so much a question of discovering the meaning of a given Old Testament passage as of finding there a confirmation of one's position, and of demonstrating the historical continuity between the Old and New Testaments.

According to this, then, the aim of interpretations of the Old Testament in the New is not so much to investigate the exact literal sense of the Old Testament passages as to invoke the support of the Old Testament by using the methods of interpreting the sacred text which were then in force. And if this is indeed the case, then the only question which can justifiably be put is whether this was, in principle, the correct course for the New Testament authors to take.

In view of the fact that the Old Testament is, in many respects, a presentation of the history that leads up to the making of the new covenant, and that the latter without the former is inconceivable, this reference to the past was a necessity for Christians. The fact that the methods used to accomplish it were bound up with one particular period is something that follows from the fact that the old and new covenants are themselves bound up with history. New Testament interpretation of the Old Testament had much in common with the allegorizing methods of exegesis prevalent during the early ages of the Church, and also in mediaeval times. By the standards of scriptural interpretation used by the Jews and by these interpreters of the Patristic and mediaeval ages the interpretation of the Old Testament in the New had appeared quite normal. But in modern times, once the above-

[27] H. Renard, "La lecture de l'Ancien Testament par Saint Paul", *Studiorum Paulinorum Congressus Internationalis Catholicus 1961,* vol. II (1963), pp. 207–15.
[28] J. A. Fitzmyer, "OT Quotations in Qumran Lit. and NT", pp. 306 ff., 330 f.

mentioned standards had ceased to carry any weight, the validity of the New Testament interpretations of Old Testament passages, a subject which had long been regarded as raising no problems, was called in question.[29] While the methods of interpreting the Old Testament used in the New can no longer be considered to have absolute validity for all purposes and at all times, still it must be noticed that however circumscribed these methods may have been by the interests of a particular epoch, the principal cause for using them survives and continues in force. This fact is implicit in the claim that Old and New Testament alike are true in a special sense. In this case too the axiom applies that 'the baby must not be thrown out with the bath-water'; by the way in which they interpret Old Testament passages the authors of the New Testament bear witness to the fact that the God who has manifested his faithfulness ('true-ness') in the Old Testament, that same God has remained faithful in the New.[30] In this sense the New Testament interpretation of Old Testament passages continues to be true and to present us with a valid model.

Viewed from the standpoint of the biblical concept of truth, therefore, the theory of the *sensus plenior* involves a conception of truth which is on a different plane, and which is foreign to the Bible itself, so that it can hardly be regarded as a solution to the problem of how the Old and New Testaments are connected. But it is not merely from this standpoint of the biblical concept of truth that objections are to be raised against the *sensus plenior*

[29] J. Schmid, "Die alttestamentl. Zitate bei Paulus und die Theorie vom sensus plenior", p. 162; cf. further G. von Rad, *Theologie des Alten Testamentes,* vol. II, p. 380.

[30] According to Paul the faithfulness of God is the central factor for the connection between the Old and New Testaments, Israel and the Church. Cf. H. Müller, "Die Auslegung alttestamentlichen Geschichtsstoffes bei Paulus", *TLZ* 86 (1961), cols. 788–9; J. Bligh, "The Church and Israel according to St. John and St. Paul", *Studiorum Paulinorum Congressus Internationalis Catholicus 1961,* vol. I (1963), pp. 151–6; J. Coppens, "Les arguments scripturaires et leur portée dans les lettres pauliniennes", *Studiorum Paulinorum Congressus Internationalis Catholicus 1961,* vol. II (1963), p. 250.

theory. We arrive at the same conclusion on more general grounds, namely by taking cognizance of the peculiar quality of literary creations, among which the writings of the Bible are all without exception to be numbered.

The writings of the Old and New Testaments have this in common with all other literatures that they constitute an objective fact of social history.[31] Thus they stand in a twofold relationship to the human community from which they have emerged. First these writings are related to the particular generation of that community which was alive when they were composed. Let us call this relationship *synchronistic*. It means that the language in which the writings were composed was the language which was then living and current among the composers' own contemporaries. It follows that these contemporaries of the composers must, to some extent at least, have been able to understand their work. Second the writings are related to one particular human group or nation throughout all its history, and including all the generations of that group both preceding and following upon the particular generation among which the authors of the writings are numbered. Let us call this relationship *diachronistic*. It means that the works themselves have a connection with the past and the future. They are connected with the past in the sense that in respect of the questions which are raised, the language that is used and the subjects which are treated of[32] they are dependent upon the earlier literature.[33] In this way the New Testament

---

[31] Cf. H. Lausberg, *Handbuch der literarischen Rhetorik* (Index volume) (1960), p. 946.

[32] The problem of the *topoi* in contemporary literary thought is new; for this reason many aspects of it await further clarification. Cf. W. Veit, "Toposforschung. Ein Forschungsbericht", *Deutsche Vierteljahrsschrift für Literaturwissenschaft und Geistesgeschichte* 37 (1963), pp. 120–63.

[33] A. Gehlen, *Der Mensch. Seine Natur und seine Stellung in der Welt* (5th ed., 1955), p. 332, points out that "a major achievement of speech and knowledge consists precisely in the fact that it places earlier experiences at the service of the *future*, so that they do not have to be investigated and traced back to their origins *all over again* each time they occur". Gehlen continues, therefore:

stands in a complex 'diachronistic' relationship to the Old, in virtue of the fact that it is the work of a later generation of the same distinct human group.[34] But in addition to the 'diachronistic' connection which has just been described, there is a second one, namely this: the Old Testament is 'diachronistically' connected with the New in virtue of the fact that, regarded as an entire compositum, it has a future orientation towards the New Testament.[35] According to Aristotle the orientation of a literary work

"Henceforward we always adopt a position towards the events which is determined by our 'basis of historical reaction', without having to run through the whole catalogue of problems each time we encounter one of them, and with the basic possibility of falling into subjectivism."

[34] See, for example, B. S. Schulz, "Markus und das Alte Testament", *ZTK* 58 (1961), pp. 184–97.

[35] In his article, "Das Alte Testament in der Dogmatik", *Gedenkschrift für D. W. Elert* (1955), pp. 272–82 W. Trillhaas investigates the fact that since Schleiermacher and the idealist philosophers a whole series of leading Protestant theologians has emerged (among those of the twentieth century W. Herrmann and A. von Harnack should especially be mentioned), who no longer ascribe any significant role to the Old Testament. Trillhaas accuses the exponents of this approach (cf. pp. 280–2) of having failed to realize that the commandment of love constitutes the very heart and centre of the law, and also that man becomes a sinner by the law, although the law was given for life: "He wishes to lead the people by the law. The law is the consolation of the people (cf. Ps. 119:92). The law that accuses us is, at the same time, an expression of divine grace" (*ibid.*, p. 280). Trillhaas further regards the uniqueness of the Old Testament as "consisting in the fact that it sets the origins of human guilt firmly in the origins of human history" (*ibid.*, p. 281). The third point at which, as Trillhaas holds, the significance of the Old Testament goes beyond that of a mere historical preamble to the New Testament is in the portrayal of man which emerges from it. Corresponding to this Old Testament portrayal of man is the portrayal of God which, so Trillhaas contends, differs from that offered by the philosophers in four respects: first, the vitality of God, whom man can only apprehend by experiencing him in act, second, the fact that man can know him only by faith, third that he can know what his grace means only by substituting the experience of self-surrender to God for the experience of sin, fourth that everything attested by the Old Testament concerning God in "its depths as well as its weaknesses, it owes to history" (*ibid.*, p. 282).

towards the future is determined by its 'καθόλου-character'. Aristotle ascribes this to poetry.[36] Here the 'καθόλου-character' is based upon the message of the poem considered as an integral whole: according to him poetry is more philosophical in character, and richer in content than history, for poetry expresses that which is universal and comprehensive whereas history presents only individual facts.[37] Can this theory of the Greek philosopher be applied to the relationship between the Old and the New Testaments in view of the fact that it is precisely history that is accorded so significant a part in these writings?

The essential point is that the orientation towards the future intended by the author (which is 'diachronistic' in the sense explained above) should exist. It is in fact objectively present in the writings of the Old Testament. For the intention of these is to point to that which is transcendent and universal in the life of Israel, that which has been made real and effective in the covenant; and in pointing to the making of the covenant in the past they intend also to remind their fellow Israelites of the obligations which it lays upon them in the present and future. The books of the Old Testament speak of a *faithfulness* and a love on God's part which knows no limits and which, whatever the situation, never arrives at a point when it is exhausted or comes to an end. The realm of the future always remains greater than that of the past or the present. That which is universal and permanent in the life of Israel becomes effective in the covenant in many ways,[38] for the covenant shapes the entire life of the people. It follows that the

---

[36] Cf. Lausberg, *Handbuch der literarischen Rhetorik,* p. 559.

[37] See J.-E. Heyde, "Διὸ ποίησις καὶ φιλοσοφώτερον καὶ σπουδαιότερον ἱστορίας ἐστίν; Aristoteles, Poetik c q (1451 b 6). Ein Beitrag zur Geschichte des Wortes φιλοσοφία" in G. Erdmann and A. Eichstaedt, eds., *Worte und Werte. B. Markwardt zum 60. Geburtstag* (1961), pp. 123–41.

[38] How far the form of the all-embracing event, in which every being is inserted into the temporal order, finds expression here in the historical life of Israel taken as a whole, is a question apart. On the philosophical problem involved here cf. R. Schaeffler, *Die Struktur der Geschichtszeit* (1963), pp. 545 ff.

writings of the Old Testament, which give an account of this present life, no less than works of poetry — and here we should notice the prominent place accorded to poetry in the Old Testament writings — are never made out of date by historical developments. So far as their *voluntas,* the intention latent in them, is concerned, the writings of the Old Testament always continue to be living, for the history which they describe as leading up to the covenant, and the promises which they proclaim as belonging to it, are determined in their form by the covenant itself. They have not yet arrived at their *total consummation* even if they have attained a *fulfilment* in the New Testament.

While the all-embracing 'καθόλου-character' of a work can cause it to survive and continue as a living entity in this way, it must further be noted that the meaning of a given piece of writing can be shown in a new light by historical developments and by the changing of situations. The forces that become effective in language transcend the immediate purpose of the individual writer,[39] and only the future can fully reveal the ultimate force and significance latent in a given piece of writing.[40] For this reason it is misleading to speak of a 'deeper' sense, or a 'full' sense. Thus the artificiality of the so-called *sensus plenior* stands revealed; in the last analysis it is based on a devaluation of the literal sense, and takes too little account of the general laws of human language.[41] The fresh consideration which arises here — probably only when

[39] In his book, *Das sprachliche Kunstwerk* (7th ed., 1961), pp. 225 f., W. Kayser shows that the author does not necessarily recognize the significance of his work. The same also applies to his contemporaries.

[40] History cannot be regarded as an enclosed sphere; thus the future is always integrally bound up with it, and the interpretation of a passage of Scripture is never so complete as to be incapable of further development. Cf. J. Moltmann, "Exegese und Eschatologie der Geschichte", p. 59. On the question of how the effects produced by a piece of writing influence its interpretation cf. H.-G. Gadamer, *Wahrheit und Methode* (1960), pp. 284 ff.

[41] In his article, "Hermeneutics in the Light of Language and Literature", *CBQ* 25 (1963), pp. 371–86, L. Alonso-Schökel rightly insists that in interpreting Scripture the general rules of hermeneutics must be observed.

we have discarded views on human language which, though antiquated, still tend to influence our judgments — is that it is a basic and universal characteristic of human language that it is orientated towards the future;[42] and this has to be taken into account particularly in its bearing upon the relationship between the Old and New Testaments.

We have spoken above of a two-fold survival and continuance of Old Testament passages in the New Testament, and in consequence in Christian life as well. From what has been said it will now be apparent that this is the result of the making of the cove-

---

[42] A. Gehlen, in his book, *Der Mensch. Seine Natur und seine Stellung in der Welt*, pp. 313–41, refers to the basic connection with the future which is inherent in speech and truth. With Gehlen it must be said that the further significance and import of a statement is determined by its primary meaning (*ibid.*, p. 323), and that "the third 'element of meaning' in truth" consists in its capacity for further implications and further effectiveness with reference to the future. With Gehlen it must further be observed: "A further, and no less radical element of irrationality lies at the *social* level of our nature, with its proneness to communication, the influence of one mind upon another and imitation. We receive innumerable communications and suggestions, with the result that our judgments are based upon the attitudes and experiences of *others*, and are seldom derived from those which we have accumulated for ourselves. Hence it is only in the sphere of genuinely scientific and empirical thought that we can to some extent achieve a significant degree of abstraction from the social milieu; we do not achieve this in those subjects which are matters of broad experience and the meanings of which are evident to all, for the experience which we call our own in such matters is to a large extent the experience of others. It is in this sense that we should understand an extremely penetrating remark of Karl Vossler (*Geist und Kultur in der Sprache*, 1925), to the effect that when an idea or a theory appears on the horizon it is not so much that idea in itself that becomes known and is transmitted to others, but rather the congeries of human thoughts and feelings that lies behind it. It must be stated that besides the sense which a statement bore as it came from the lips of its original author — one thinks of the meanings contained in the Sermon on the Mount — another, and very different one may come to be attached to it. This is the sense in which the statement in question has been received, understood and transmitted by others. Now the historical meaning of the statement is not so much the sense which it was originally intended to

nant and of the special history thereby inaugurated.[43] It follows that it is also the result of God's being 'true' in the sense of faithful to his word.

In this connection a further point must be observed. The connection between word and deed on the one hand and the covenant on the other remains in its essential structure basically constant and unchanging. Because of this the history which covers the period between the making of the first covenant and the last brings us again and again to events which are 'typical' of the whole so that the Old Testament can also be interpreted 'typologically' from the standpoint of the New.[44]

The interpretation of the Old Testament in a typological sense in the New is to be regarded as justifiable to the extent that by this method, which is universally practised, significant factors are pointed to. Typology makes it possible to render the past fruitful for the present. It brings out its significance for life in the

bear once and for all as the dynamic effectiveness which it acquires from the latter point of view" (*ibid.*, p. 333).

In my opinion these observations of Gehlen lead to the general conclusion that the problem of the 'pregnancy' of language, that is its capacity to have further meanings educed from it in the future, is to be explained initially from the nature of language itself. Only when this has been done can we then go on to assess the responsibility of God as the *auctor primarius* for the alleged *sensus plenior*. To make God responsible for this is possible only if we presuppose a distinction between natural and supernatural which has already been determined beforehand, and which has had a narrowly defined interpretation placed upon it.

[43] Cf. G. von Rad, *Theologie des Alten Testaments,* vol. II, pp. 381 f., 396.
[44] On the history of Jewish-Christian typology see L. Goppelt, *Typos. Die Deutung des Alten Testaments im Neuen* (1939); F. Hesse, H. Nakagawa, E. Fascher, "Typologie", *RGG* VI (1962), cols. 1094–8; L. Goppelt, "Apokalyptik und Typologie bei Paulus", *TLZ* 89 (1964), col. 339, rightly emphasizes that the true and objectively based connection between the two Testaments is to be sought in the New Testament presentation of the faithfulness of God, but pays too little heed in his line of argument to the fact that typology also occurs outside Christian literature. See R. P. C. Hanson, *Allegory and Event* (1959), p. 370.

present, and in this way is designed to lead on to action.[45] It lies
in the very nature of typology that it is able to contribute towards
the elucidation and interpretation of history only within certain
well-defined limits, so that we can never arrive at a full realization
of the relationship between the Old and New Testaments in all
its complexity. Thus with regard to the relationship between the
Old and New Testaments it turns out that the historical connection between the old and new covenants is based upon God's
will to remain faithful to his people, a will that is made effective

---

[45] How far this state of affairs is already true of profane history is shown by
A. Mirgeler in his article "Erfahrung in der Geschichte und Geschichtswissenschaft", *Experiment und Erfahrung in Wissenschaft und Kunst*, p. 242 ff.:
"As we have already indicated the precise theme of a history undertaken from
this point of view is not historical truth but historical importance. Nietzsche
ascribes certain characteristics to a kind of history which he designates 'the
monumental'. It is easy to see that many of these characteristics apply to the
history with which we are here concerned. Admittedly we must straightway
take into account that what Nietzsche has in mind as a disciple of the 'Enlightenment' is not at this stage the history of the empire as such; his polemics
against the 'empire' of Bismarck are well known. But these developed not so
much from a political attitude of mind as from a hostility on a deeper plane
against all that is 'imperial'. Nietzsche's target is the man who is 'written up'
to heroic dimensions. If, for the sake of example, we assume this 'point of
view', the characteristics of 'monumental history' indicated by him will
appear appropriate and applicable to an 'imperial' history thus conceived.
According to Nietzsche it is not the past in its entirety that is recorded in
'monumental history', but only 'certain great events' which enable us to
'believe in humanity', and also certain 'individual facts carefully embellished',
such data, therefore, as will permit one to see human existence as something
exalted and something basically free from blemish. Similarly a monumental
'imperial history' does not treat of the whole of the past, but only of certain
great events which have contributed to the building up of the empire, and
which are designed to foster belief in the empire, and certain carefully embellished facts which, while they may not have so contributed, are still offered as
at most 'awful warnings' or as proof of strength that did not fail even in the
most testing circumstances.

"The underlying purpose of the 'monumental' approach to history is an
exhortatory one. This is clearly expressed by Livy in the preface to his Roman
history: 'What chiefly makes the study of history wholesome and profitable

in word and deed, yet without ever attaining its complete fulfil-ment. From a linguistic and literary point of view this fact is reflected in the books of the Bible, which describe this history with the various literary aids which were then available (Midrash, typology, etc.). Literary methods and forms of expression are not, however, identical with the truth of sacred Scripture. The attempt still had to be made, with the help of a *sensus plenior,* to even out the differences of period and to find what was later already present in what was earlier.

is this, that you behold the lessons of every kind of experience set forth as on a conspicuous monument. From these you may choose for yourself and for your own state what to imitate, from these mark for avoidance what is shameful in the conception and shameful in the result'. The morality of history which Livy here seeks to inculcate is a 'state' morality, though admittedly not a totalitarian one imposed by the state, but one to be made real by the impetus and effort of its citizens. But the means by which this impetus is to be aroused is praise of a past which is 'written up' to heroic dimensions. For this reason we shall no longer speak in what follows of a 'monumental history' but of a 'panegyric history', because this term 'pan-ageiro' expresses the reference to a state in its totality which is to be built up by means of this kind of praise."

From the standpoint of philosophy M. Scheler has taken up and explored the idea of example, and shown that it plays a decisive part in human life. See Max Scheler, *Gesammelte Werke,* vol. X (1957), pp. 257–344. In his essay "Vom Wirkungsgeheimnis des menschengestaltigen Gottes", *Erlanger Beiträge zur Sprach- und Kunstwissenschaft* 7 (1960), pp. 205–52, C. Koch brings us to a fresh awareness of the depths and significance which we should ascribe to the axiom *Verba docent, exempla trahunt.* On example in the New Testament A. Schulz has recently made a contribution in his book, *Nachfolgen und Nach-ahmen. Studien über das Verhältnis der neutestamentlichen Jüngerschaft zur urchrist-lichen Vorbildethik* (1962); id., "Leidenstheologie und Vorbildethik in den paulinischen Hauptbriefen", *Neutestamentliche Aufsätze — Festschrift J. Schmid* (1963), pp. 265–9; for a fresh re-appraisal of the place of typology in the historical sciences and exegesis cf. R. Wittram, *Das Interesse an der Geschichte* (2nd ed., 1963), pp. 46 ff.; G. von Rad, *Theologie des Alten Testamentes,* vol. II, pp. 381 f.; J. Moltmann, "Exegese und Eschatologie der Geschichte", p. 61; P. Grelot, *Sens chrétien de l'Ancien Testament* (1962), pp. 25 ff., 214 ff. With regard to the typological interpretation of the Bible and its effect on the development of European literature Erich Auerbach's works on figurative interpretation should be noticed. Auerbach investigates the question of how we should

Finally one further word must be said here[46] about the connection between revelation and covenant people. God's act of self-revelation took place in the course of making the covenant. For this reason there is a permanent bond between revelation and people of God. Since the purpose of revelation is the forging of a life-giving relationship between God and his people this relationship has, amongst other aspects, an ecclesiological one — corresponding to the ἐκκλησία of the old and new covenants.[47] By the covenant the Lord formed his own people,[48] which testifies to the world concerning the God who has been revealed to them[49] by living according to his will as their covenant Lord, and by the life and the abiding place in history which God has bestowed upon them. The people who owe their survival to God's faithfulness to his covenant thus bear witness by the very fact of their existence to revealed truth, and direct the eyes of mankind to God who has revealed himself.

But any member of the people of God who does not live according to the vocation which God has given him sets obstacles

understand the typological interpretation of the Bible and defines figurative interpretation as follows: "Figurative interpretation 'establishes a connection between two events or persons in such a way that the first signifies not only itself but also the second, while the second involves or fulfils the first. The two poles of a figure are separated in time, but both, being real events or persons, are within temporality. They are both contained in the flowing stream, which is historical life, and only the comprehension, the *intellectus spiritualis*, of their interdependence is a spiritual act.' In practice we almost always find an interpretation of the Old Testament, whose episodes are interpreted as figures or phenomenal prophecies of the events of the New Testament" (E. Auerbach, *Mimesis. The Representation of Reality in Western Literature* [1953], p. 64).

[46] Cf. ch. iv.

[47] Cf., amongst others, W. Bulst, *Offenbarung* (1960), pp. 97–101; T. Rendtorff, "Das Offenbarungsproblem im Kirchenbegriff", *KDB* 1, pp. 115–31.

[48] H. Wildberger, *Jahwes Eigentumsvolk* (1960), pp. 113 ff.

[49] With regard to the ecclesiological aspect of revelation our earlier observations on the hidden character of revelation (cf. p. 120, n. 9) must be borne in mind.

in the path by which others may arrive at the revealed truth. Hence Paul's reproach to the Jews, who boast that the law belongs to them and yet transgress it: "As it is written (cf. Is 52:5, LXX), the name of God is blasphemed among the Gentiles because of you" (Rom 2:24).

In conclusion it must be said that the special claim to veracity of Scripture provides the basis for the claim to absolute truth of Christianity and the Bible. God has created a bond between himself and his people, which is indissoluble, of a unique kind, unrepeatable and embracing all men. What this bond is designed to achieve is the life of men with God. Thus the claim to absolute truth in no sense provides grounds for maintaining that the Bible has a special superiority in the spheres of politics or of intellectual or cultural pursuits, or a pre-eminent place in literature.

Vatican II. The only revelation of God spoken of in *Dei Verbum* is one whose truth applies to all and which advances towards a final consummation. "The Christian dispensation, therefore, as the new and definitive covenant, will never pass away, and we now await no further new public revelation before the glorious manifestation of our Lord Jesus Christ" (Ch. I, art. 4). It is of the nature of this revelation that while it is orientated towards a point at which it will ultimately be verified by God, it is initially bestowed in history and under historical conditions. In consequence this historical revelation of God is not necessarily recognized as such by mankind; it is not evident irresistibly with the force of a mathematical demonstration. Man is directed towards the grace of God: "If this faith is to be shown, the grace of God and the interior help of the Holy Spirit must precede and assist, moving the heart and turning it to God, opening the eyes of the mind and giving 'joy and ease to everyone assenting to the truth and believing it'. To bring about an ever deeper understanding of revelation the same Holy Spirit constantly brings faith to completion by his gifts" (Ch. I, art. 5).

It must be noticed in particular that in *Dei Verbum* no decision is to be found for or against the *sensus plenior* theory. The Council was not able to take up any decisive position on this point.[50]

[50] Cf. *Schema Constitutionis de Divina Revelatione* (1964), p. 31: "Abstrahitur autem a solvenda quaestione de 'sensu pleniore'." *Schema Constitutionis Dogmaticae de Divina Revelatione. Modi a patribus conciliaribus propositi a Commissione Doctrinali examinati* (1965), p. 35: "Pag. 22, lin. 1: Tredecim Patres petunt ut, loco et, scribatur quidque, ut appareat quaestionem de sensu pleniore non dirimi. R. — Omnes concordant de non dirimenda hac questione. Si scribitur quidque, quaestio in sensum positivum dirimeretur. Expressio et est neutralis."

CHAPTER EIGHT

FURTHER CONSIDERATIONS ON TRUTH
IN THE BIBLE

> Madame de Volanges to Madame de Rosemonde:
> "I now experience the fact that our understanding,
> which is, in any case, insufficient to avert our misfortune,
> is still more inadequate to bring us consolation."
>
> Paris, 14th January, 17 . .
>
> "All flesh is grass . . .
> The grass withers, the flower fades;
> but the word of our God will stand for ever."
>
> Is 40:6–8.

In the earlier chapters of this study we attempted to elucidate the following thesis: the change of outlook which has established itself since the inauguration of the modern age, leads us to recognize an important fact concerning the doctrine of the absolute inerrancy of the biblical writings as upheld in the schools of Christian theology. This has been shown to be in contradiction to other conclusions which have been confirmed since the trial of Galileo. The way does, however, lie open to a solution if we revert to the biblical sources themselves. It is evident that as in other respects so too for the question of the truth of the Bible sacred Scripture is to be understood as an historical document written in human language. It is of central importance here to apprehend the nature of the Semitic and biblical concept of truth.[1]

---

[1] Regarded from the historical and philological standpoint, all such theories of absolute inerrancy remain ultimately unconvincing, and are now seen to be not in conformity with *Dei Verbum*. For the solution which they offer to the problem of the truth of the Bible is too abstract to be in conformity with the historical facts, and is based on a predetermined concept of revelation (thus probably P. Grelot, *Bible et théologie* [1965], pp. 115 f.). Alternatively they devote all their energies to demonstrating the continuity between the papal encyclicals on the Bible and *Dei Verbum,* and in this process incur the danger

It is quite basic to our understanding of the struggle concerning biblical inerrancy to realize that in the course of history the question of the truth of Scripture has come to be considered and treated of in categories of thought which are foreign to Scripture itself. A decisive factor here, and one which, moreover, orientated the whole discussion in one specific direction, was the influence of the great Augustine.[2] His philosophical and theological views led him to exaggerate the 'divine' element in the Bible at the expense of the 'human' one. "The transference of the categories 'temporal-eternal' to sacred Scripture could not but lead him willy-nilly to a similar kind of 'subtle Docetism' as in his Christology."[3]

This influence of the African Doctor of the Church persisted throughout the Middle Ages, and since then has continued to survive right up to the present. We have only to recall here the

of interpreting *Dei Verbum* in a manner contrary to its true sense — always under the influence of the *sine ullo errore* theory (cf., e.g., O. Semmelroth and M. Zerwick, *Vaticanum II über das Wort Gottes,* Stuttgarter Bibelstudien 16 (1966), p. 33: "It would be going altogether too far, and, moreover, would be contrary to the footnotes to the conciliar text, with their reference to the earlier papal encyclicals, if we were to conclude that by its new formula the Council had given positive recognition to the following theory: in Scripture certain statements are to be found which, while from the aspect of their religious content and their contribution to the salvific message of Scripture taken as a whole, could certainly not be described as errors, but which, considered from the point of view of profane history, are errors. On the other hand it would be equally untrue to say that such a possibility is now positively excluded."   [2] Cf. above, p. 3, note 8.

[3] G. Strauss, *Schriftgebrauch, Schriftauslegung und Schriftbeweis bei Augustin* (1959), p. 63. On the connection between time and eternity in Augustine see W. Veit, *Studien zur Geschichte des Topos der goldenen Zeit von der Antike bis zum 18. Jahrhundert* (Dissertation, Univ. of Cologne, 1961); id., "Toposforschung. Ein Forschungsbericht", *Deutsche Vierteljahrsschrift für Literaturwissenschaft und Geistesgeschichte* 37 (1963), p. 153. R. Schaeffler provides a penetrating analysis of the problem of time in Augustine in his *Die Struktur der Geschichtszeit* (1963), pp. 188–238. Not only Augustine but Origen also was influenced by Philo in his views on the inerrancy of Scripture. See R. P. C. Hanson, *Allegory and Event* (1959), pp. 191 ff., 368.

expositions of Aquinas,[4] John Duns Scotus,[5] Melchior Cano,[6] Suárez,[7] and more recent studies in dogmatic theology.[8]

Regarded as a whole the intellectual changes at the outset of the modern age signify a turning to experience and experiment, and they dominate our present view of the world and our attitude to life. But they could not be otherwise than most sharply opposed to the teaching on the truth of Scripture which was influenced by Augustine. The insuperable 'misunderstanding'[9] between Jerome, the philologist and Augustine the theologian had already given warning of what was to come. And now this grew into an intellectual crisis of the utmost magnitude. In this the initial impulse came from the field of astronomy.

Thus the effect of the advent of the Copernican system in Europe is that "the place of the Bible is radically changed. Exact

[4] I a, q. 68, a. 1; II–II, q. 171, a. 6 c; Quodl. 12, q. 16, a. 26 ad 1; *In Johannem Evangelistam* 13, lect. 1; U. Horst, "Das Wesen der 'auctoritas' nach Thomas von Aquin", *MTZ* 13 (1962), p. 165, on Ia 8 ad 2.

[5] J. Finkenzeller, *Offenbarung und Theologie nach der Lehre des Johannes Duns Skotus* (1961), pp. 42 f.

[6] *De locis theologicis* II c. 3–4. On the earlier history of the *loci theologici* see A. Lang, *Die Entfaltung des apologetischen Problems in der Scholastik des Mittelalters* (1962), p. 206, n. 20.

[7] *Tract. de Fide, de Regulis Fidei,* Disp. 5, 3, 3.

[8] C. Pesch, *De Inspiratione Sacrae Scripturae* (1925), pp. 489 ff.; Diekamp-Jüssen, *Katholische Dogmatik nach den Grundsätzen des heiligen Thomas,* vol. I (13th ed., 1958), p. 40.

[9] Cf. Strauss, *Schriftgebrauch,* pp. 61 f. This is not to say that in his views on the inerrancy of Scripture Jerome differs in any essentials from Augustine. But what separates him from Augustine is that he is unable to be so ready with logical answers to the problems involved as Augustine. Thus cf. L. Schade, *Die Inspirationslehre des heiligen Hieronymus* (1910), pp. 82 f. With reference to the dispute between Augustine and Jerome concerning Paul's behaviour at Antioch this author comes to the conclusion that: "It is established, then, beyond dispute that in the view of our two fathers of the Church Paul was guilty of a white lie; so far as he is concerned, then, apostolicity does not appear to provide any guaranteed basis for inspiration and inerrancy. On the other hand when we enquire into the motives for this unfortunate attempt at a solution then we must admit that it was precisely their efforts to rule out any

science has greater power to convey truth than the Bible. This position, initiated by the victory of the Copernican system, gradually comes to be regarded as self-evident by all Europeans. A necessary corollary of this is that for practical purposes the Bible is no longer treated as without qualification and in all its aspects a divine book. The saecular awareness of truth rebels against the restrictions of religion and conquers them."[10] The authority of the Bible having once been radically shaken from the side of natural science, subsequently declines still more in men's estimation as a source of truth because of the development of other disciplines in the fields of philology and history.[11] The Bible ceases to be the book which gives an accurate account of the history of humanity. Its claim that knowledge of the world shall proceed from it and be orientated to it grows progressively

contradiction between the two apostles and to find an underlying agreement between their views, extremely divergent though they appear to have been, that caused them to resort to this desperate expedient. Again, Paul himself had to be safeguarded against the accusation that at Antioch he spoke in a manner which could not be reconciled with his earlier behaviour. Thus Jerome rescues one principle by a blatant violation of it!" In practice neither Augustine not Jerome achieved a satisfactory solution to the problem on the basis of their theories.

[10] E. Hirsch, *Geschichte der neuern evangelischen Theologie im Zusammenhang mit den allgemeinen Bewegungen des europäischen Denkens,* vol. I (1949), p. 204. It is becoming recognized more and more that the turn to experimentalism is also the outcome of certain specific philosophical presuppositions; see G. Wolandt, "Die moderne Grundlegungstheorie und der Galileische Naturbegriff", *Philosophia naturalis* 8 (1964), pp. 191–7. For an understanding of the modern controversy over the authority of the Bible an investigation into the influence of the Roman concept of authority upon Christian theology would be necessary. On the question of authority see R. Heinze, "Auctoritas", *Vom Geist des Römertums. Ausgewählte Aufsätze* (3rd ed., 1960), pp. 43–58; on the history of the authority of the Bible in Luther and Protestantism see H. Ostergaard-Nielsen, *Scriptura sacra et viva vox* (1957), pp. 19–28; R. Hermann, *Von der Klarheit der Heiligen Schrift* (1958); J. K. S. Reid, *The Authority of Scripture* (1962), pp. 11–102; H. D. McDonald, *Theories of Revelation* (1963), pp. 288–346.

[11] *Ibid.,* pp. 222 ff.

weaker. The harmony between Scripture and Greek philosophy which Philo[12] strove to achieve, and which was subsequently taken over by the fathers as far as possible, is radically and conclusively called in question. What up till now has been a 'heritage of truth' held in common by Christians, Jews and in part Mohammedans is subjected to annihilating criticisms. The biblical account of the history of mankind prior to Moses, and of the course of events after the exodus, is rejected as unreliable. Since Philo's time the orthodox have loved to 'prove' the truth of the divine origin of the law and the teaching of the prophets by having recourse to arguments such as the miracles performed by the prophets, the prophetic traditions of the future, the Sinai revelation and the grandeur inherent in the law and the teaching of the prophets. Now this line of argument is rejected as unworthy of belief.

In what light should this development be regarded from the point of view of Scripture and the Church? As in other branches of theology, so here too the course of events forces us to consider Scripture more closely, and to decide what really is binding in the teaching of the Church. A return to the statements concerning truth contained in the Bible itself enables us to realize that in no sense does Scripture itself claim to be inerrant in Augustine's sense of the term. The Semitic and Hebrew concept of truth lays the accent on 'true' in the sense of 'faithful'. Measured by this concept of truth Scripture would be in error if God were to act unfaithfully, and if, as a result, what is asserted in Scripture concerning God's faithfulness was unmasked and shown to be a lie. The developments of the modern age, therefore, have had the effect of making us examine the statements in Scripture itself concerning its claim to veracity instead of substituting alien views for those statements.

More confusing than the way in which Scripture is represented

[12] On the position of Philo see H. A. Wolfson, *Religious Philosophy* (1961), pp. 217 ff. ("The Veracity of Scripture from Philo to Spinoza").

in the question of biblical veracity is the way in which the teaching of the Church is represented. The effect of the general developments in the field of thought has been that at the First Council of the Vatican (Vatican I) an explicit, conciliar and doctrinal statement on inspiration — and so too on the question of the veracity of Scripture — was finally arrived at. For here the following statement is made concerning the books of the Bible: "These books are held by the Church as sacred and canonical not as having been composed by merely human labour and afterwards approved by her authority, nor merely because they contain revelation without error, but because, written under the inspiration of the Holy Ghost, they have God for their author and have been transmitted to the Church as such.[13]

It is striking that the Council's formula is: '. . . *quod revelationem sine errore contineant*'. Thus Vatican I refrains absolutely from applying the phrase *sine errore* to Scripture itself in any respect at all. The Council attaches this *sine errore* to the *revelatio* which is contained in Scripture. It is further to be noted that what is achieved is that all error is excluded from the *revelatio*; in other words we have only a negative statement before us. The Council has refrained from mentioning any individual passages of Scripture as authorities by which the inerrancy of the Bible is to stand or fall. The Council has been able to forego any positive formulation, for it is possible to find a solution to the problem of truth that goes into the particular details on the basis of Scripture and the tradition of the Church even without a dogmatic definition. The statement of the Council on the question of the truth of Scripture confines itself to what is most important, and must be described as a prudent and — from the point of view of Scripture itself — a fortunate one.[14]

In more recent presentations connected with the problem of

---

[13] *EB,* p. 77.
[14] Up till the present it has proved impossible to refuse this interpretation of the statement of Vatican I, which has received general assent. Cf., for example, I. de la Potterie in *NRT* 98 (1966), p. 160.

scriptural inerrancy a tendency can be discerned which is in harmony with the teaching of Vatican I. The authors concerned tend to distinguish between the content of a statement and its form, and to claim inerrancy only for the first of these.[15] On this differentiation M. Schmaus remarks: "The distinction is not to be understood in the sense that orthodox teaching has to some extent been rendered pliable in the face of the conclusions of the natural science of modern times, as though the literal sense of sacred Scripture had been abandoned or even watered down. On the contrary, the point of the distinction is to penetrate to the real sense of sacred Scripture, and to separate it from a sense which adheres slavishly to the meanings of individual words. The real meaning is only arrived at when we ask ourselves the question 'What does sacred Scripture itself mean to say?'"[16]

To arrive at this position is, as we have already mentioned,[17] to touch upon the central problem of the inerrancy of sacred Scripture itself. The distinction referred to by Schmaus cannot in fact be considered as a 'watering down' of the Church's teaching on the innerancy of the Bible. At the same time it does represent a *certain* yielding in the face of the conclusions of the natural science of modern times to the extent that the earlier ideal of Scripture as an absolutely perfect book has been abandoned. A further point which has rightly been observed is that the form in which the books of the Bible are presented cannot provide any criterion for deciding the question of the truth of Scripture. The phenomenon of literary categories is to be found in all literatures, and cannot therefore be invoked as a way of solving definitively the special problem of biblical inerrancy. All that is claimed to be free from error is, therefore, 'What sacred Scripture itself means to say',[18] or, to state this in the terms employed by Vatican I: '. . . *quod revelationem sine errore contineant*'. But we have then to investigate, taking the biblical concept of truth as our guide,

---

[15] M. Schmaus, *Katholische Dogmatik,* vol. I (6th ed., 1960), pp. 128 f.
[16] *Ibid.,* pp. 129 f.   [17] *Ibid.*   [18] *Ibid.*

what kind of inerrancy is claimed for this *revelatio* contained in Scripture.

It should be noticed that no argument can be adduced either from the tradition of the Church or from Scripture which would oblige anyone to accept as *de fide* any Augustinian interpretation of scriptural inerrancy, or of the declaration of Vatican I concerning scriptural inerrancy. In view of this fact the Augustinian teaching upon this point can be abandoned.

We, on the other hand, find ourselves in the happy position of receiving positive assistance from Vatican I precisely because its carefully calculated formulation points the way to a genuine understanding of the question of truth in the Bible, and thereby contributes to surmounting the problem. And now Vatican II carries the line taken by Vatican I still further, and by 'playing down' the *sine ullo errore* theory opens the way to a definitive solution: the truth claimed for sacred Scripture is to be understood in the sense of the Semitic and biblical concept of truth. The question is not 'Does sacred Scripture contain errors?' or 'Is it immune to error?' but rather: 'What truth does sacred Scripture teach us without a lie (inerrantly)?' In this respect Vatican II can claim the honour of being the first since the trial of Galileo to enter positively into questions which have remained unanswered for more than three hundred years. In view of the influence and authority of the *sine ullo errore* theory, still upheld in official circles, it can be understood that the process by which the Council can give full effect to its teaching can only be a slow one.

Even outside the restricted context of the doctrine of inspiration the adoption of a concept of truth that is foreign to Semitic thought has necessarily led to difficulties. This is especially true of the question of the infallibility of the Church and of the Pope.

The current discussion of infallibility enables us to realize forcibly that the concept of infallibility is a disputed one.[19] For

[19] Cf., e.g., H. Küng, *Strukturen der Kirche* (1962), pp. 309 ff., E. T.: *Structures of the Church* (1963); id., "L'Infaillibilité de l'Église", *Collection Irénikon* (1963).

147

this reason it has already been suggested that the phrase 'freedom from error' (inerrancy) should be used in place of 'infallibility'.[20]

It could also be to the advantage of theology in dealing with this question to ponder carefully the fundamental meaning of the statements in Scripture concerning God's 'true-ness' in the sense of 'faithfulness', for in this way a better view could be maintained of the broader context in which the specific problems of infallibility are to be regarded, especially as it is important precisely here to avoid falsifying prejudices. For theological considerations about infallibility as a phenomenon of the Church and of the successor of Peter we must take as our basis the recognition that the infallibility of the people of God derives its special character from the unique event of the covenant and the history thereby inaugurated, and that the nature of this infallibility is fundamentally determined by the Semitic concept of truth.

It follows from the special nature of the covenant between God and Israel that the faithfulness pledged by God to his people cannot be extended to contexts which are not covered by the covenant. For instance God did not promise his effective support, and thereby 'infallibility', to the covenant people of either the Old Testament or the New in the contexts of natural science or politics.

The collection of these works in a single series illustrates extremely well the current confusion as to what is to be understood by infallibility. A characteristic of all the works is their *de facto* disregard of Scripture. Cf. e.g. B. K. Herbst, "Die Unfehlbarkeit der fehlbaren Kirche", *Una Sancta* 18 (1963), pp. 248–62. On the history of the concept of the infallibility of the Church and the discussion of this in Vatican I cf. F. van der Horst, *Das Schema über die Kirche auf dem I. Vatikanischen Konzil* (1963), pp. 257–90. Among the representatives of the new theology, I. Ottiger, *Theologia fundamentalis*, vol. II (1911), pp. 274–377, provides the most comprehensive treatment of the problem of the 'infallibility' of the Church known to me. His whole treatise is prefixed with the title "De Perpetuitate et Immutabilitate Ecclesiae", *ibid.*, p. 274. F. A. Sullivan, *De Ecclesia*, vol. I (1963), p. 148, gives the following definition of indefectibility: "Illa Ecclesiae proprietas vi cujus ad finem mundi substantialiter eadem necessario duratura est."

[20] Küng, *Strukturen der Kirche*, p. 339.

While it is impossible for the reasons mentioned above always to expect the right decision from the people of God in every aspect of life, this should not lead us to deny that even in their practical lives they were endowed with a limited infallibility, which affected only the essentials.

For it necessarily follows from the very nature of the covenant as a pact made by God with a human group that on the human side there should always be a group of men within the people who keep faith with God, who have not bowed the knee to Baal (the 'holy remnant'). The faithfulness of God would be quite without effect if it could not raise up a band of loyal men representing the nucleus of the people. The covenant would be an illusion if the just, with their heartfelt loyalty to God, were, even for one moment, totally to disappear from the midst of either the old or the new Israel.

Here too, on the question of the infallibility of the Church, it is necessary to guard against a false intellectualism and, with regard to the errors of the Church in her conduct and practice, to come to the over-hasty conclusion that infallibility only applies to the teaching activity of the Church. If this were the case, the application of the ideal of perfection and infallibility to human activity in the moral sphere would be devoid of foundation. K. Herbst writes: "The Church is infallible in *definienda doctrina de fide vel moribus*. The departures from the gospel in the history of the Church's practical life, however grave they may be, do not affect her *infallibilitas in doctrina*. Though she cannot withdraw her *doctrina definita,* which is irrevocable, the Church is always able to reform these deviations in her practice. Certainly they are capable of rendering the Church's work to a large extent unfruitful. But they cannot destroy her nature. An example may serve to throw light upon this point: For whole centuries the Church approved of the use of physical coercion against unbelievers and heretics. In doing this she was gravely deviating in her practice from the basic intention of the gospel, yet she still remained capable of converting her ways, and *de facto* and *de jure* has with-

149

drawn from this error. Let us suppose, however, that at some single point in her history she formulated as finally conclusive and binding doctrine the following definition: 'It is the will of God revealed in Christ that recalcitrants are to be converted by force or else burned.' In this case she would have destroyed the gospel (so far as she was concerned), and, indeed, destroyed it irreparably. And this would mean that she had, in a certain sense, 'sawn through the branch on which she was sitting'; she would have destroyed herself as the Church of Christ even if, in practice, she had never persecuted heretics."[21]

What Herbst seems to have overlooked is that when the Church reforms her practice this is always achieved because of the fact that men and women live in the midst of her who by their words and deeds reject the erroneous course and so lead the way to actually changing that course; it is these that ensure that the spirit of the gospel is kept alive. History is full of examples in which God's intervention actually takes the form of employing men from outside Israel or the Church so as to awaken some kind of obedient response to the words of 'prophets' who have failed to obtain recognition among their own.[22] Isaiah stands in this sort of relationship to the Assyrians,[23] Jeremiah to Nebuchadrezzar,[24] Deutero-Isaiah to Cyrus,[25] and, so far as the people of

[21] K. Herbst, "Die Unfehlbarkeit der fehlbaren Kirche", pp. 258f.
[22] E. Buerss, "Emmanuel Hirschs Geschichte der neuern evangelischen Theologie und ihre theologische Bedeutung", *TZ* 10 (1954), p. 222: "Its [the modern world's] truth is to be found not in Kant but solely in the gospel itself. Certainly Kant can remind us of the fact that that is where it is to be found. Kant can startle us, shake us into wakefulness. Or, to speak more precisely, he can become the 'instrument' (just as once the great powers became instruments in relation to Israel) which God uses to rouse us to wakefulness."
[23] Is. 10:5.
[24] For Jeremiah the Gentile overlord Nebuchadrezzar is an instrument for the accomplishment of a universal judgment; he is called "my servant" Jer 25:9; 27:6; 43:10.
[25] In Is. 45:1, Cyrus is actually called "my anointed one". See E. Jenni, "Die

150

God is concerned, this relationship of her own prophets to out-
siders continues. The people of God is kept on the alert by prophets from within, and by the vicissitudes of history in the political and earthly sphere, so that they can find their way back to the
word of God and to his truth. The role of the Servant of God who,
by remaining true to his prophetic vocation helps the truth of God
to emerge victorious, is kept alive in the Church as well.

There is no reason, therefore, to reduce the infallibility of the
Church, problematical as it may be, to a doctrinal and dogmatic
minimum. Regarded historically, such a procedure would amount
to a last attempt to rescue that idealized concept of infallibility in
which it is identified with perfection, and is in accordance with
the essentially rationalist character of modern intellectual
movements.

At the same time it is necessary to emphasize the effects of infallibility on the spoken word (the more intellectual aspect).[26] The
pre-eminent place which the word occupies in the context of the
covenant goes back to the actual moment when it was instituted.
The covenant law provided Israel with a guiding line in the form
of words which have binding force for her. The law of the
covenant which is thus to be put into practice in the conduct of
one's life is contained in a document and consists in *words*. It is,
in fact, in every respect subject to the laws of human language,
and the problems entailed by the changing modes of human
thought. But it is in its intention that it is to be preserved. God's
faithfulness to his people, therefore, is also established by the

---

Rolle des Kyros bei Deuterojesaja", *TZ* 10 (1954), p. 242. Since Cyrus is a
willing instrument in the hand of Yahweh he is here presented in a favourable
light even though he is a Gentile overlord; see E. Fascher, "Der Vorwurf
der Gottlosigkeit in der Auseinandersetzung bei Juden, Griechen und
Christen", *Abraham unser Vater — Festschrift O. Michel* (1963), p. 101.

[26] Kinds of knowledge and truth which are speculative, and therefore also
expressed in words, are also to be found in the Church by reason of her history.
But this aspect of the life of God's people, in common with every other aspect
of the whole, is liable to misunderstanding.

fact that the guiding line for life which he imparts to them is not susceptible of any radical alternation, nor can any essential element in it be totally inverted to the opposite sense. When danger threatens, God arouses those men and women in the midst of his people, who stand out against lies. A constant struggle to preserve the purity of faith in Yahweh is apparent in the Old Testament. The covenant God will tolerate no other besides himself. At the various stages in her journey Israel must come to 'know'[27] afresh that Yahweh is her 'true' and faithful God. The threat which belief in strange gods entails is averted by a deepening of the knowledge of God through the fulfilment of his predictions. The truth concerning Yahweh is preserved in undistorted form, and in its extension to the whole human race it becomes recognized[28] as palpably present.

This same tradition is continued in the New Testament.[29] In the farewell discourse of the apostle Paul the situation of the Church is briefly delineated as follows: "I know that after my departure fierce wolves will come in among you, not sparing the flock; and from among your own selves will arise men speaking perverse things, to draw away the disciples after them" (Acts 20:29 f.). The Church must protect herself from false teachers, and hold fast to the true tradition. This the Church succeeds in doing only in virtue of the power of the Holy Ghost that has been bestowed upon her. In him she distinguishes true faith from heresy.[30]

[27] W. Zimmerli, "Erkenntnis Gottes nach dem Buche Ezechiel", *Gottes Offenbarung* (1963), pp. 54 ff.

[28] Id., "Der Wahrheitserweis Jahwes nach der Botschaft der beiden Exilspropheten", *Tradition und Situation — Festschrift A. Weiser* (1963), pp. 133 ff.

[29] H. Schürmann, "Das Testament des Paulus für die Kirche", *Unio Christianorum — Festschrift L. Jaeger* (1962), pp. 137 f.

[30] R. Bultmann, "γινώσκω", *TWNT,* vol. I, pp. 688 ff.; J. Dupont, *Gnosis. La connaissance religieuse dans les épîtres de Saint Paul* (1949); I. de la Potterie, "Oida et ginôskô, les deux modes de la connaissance dans le 4ᵉ Évangile", *Bib* 40 (1959), pp. 709–25; H. Schlier, "Glauben, Erkennen, Lieben nach dem

But while the covenant of God with his people is, of its very nature, the source of doctrinal infallibility in the Church, still it must be reiterated that even this is not to be made equivalent to perfection.[31] The words in which the 'truth' of God is formulated constitute a human and imperfect medium of expression. By being formulated in this way the truth of God resists any tendency to become 'frozen' and immobile, and so incapable of yielding any further fruit; it also resists any guarantee[32] that a given sense is plainly the ultimate one, admitting of no further development. Thus the Church can never rest content with the words in which the 'truth' is formulated, however well chosen those words may allegedly be, and anyone who favours this opinion will find that the course of history interposes a hard word of its own.

If we view the complexity of problems connected with the 'truth' of God as a whole, then it becomes clear that when Vatican I succeeded in establishing a connection between the

---

Johannesevangelium", *Einsicht und Glaube — G. Söhngen-Festschrift* (1962), pp. 102 ff.; O. Kuss, "Der Glaube nach den paulinischen Hauptbriefen", *Auslegung und Verkündigung,* vol. I (1963), p. 205: "In place of faith Paul can speak of a 'knowledge', and in fact in the same, or a similar sense. What is the matter of the preaching is grasped by the faithful in their act of believing; thenceforward it is held firm as 'knowledge' in the sense that it is the conviction which determines and guides the course of their entire lives"; H. Schlier, "Die Erkenntnis Gottes nach den Briefen des Apostels Paulus", *Gott in Welt — Festgabe für K. Rahner,* vol. I (1964), pp. 515–35.

[31] On the New Testament concept of perfection see P. J. du Plessis, *Teleios. The Idea of Perfection in the New Testament* (1959); K. Prümm, "Das neutestamentliche Sprach- und Begriffsproblem der Vollkommenheit", *Bib* 44 (1963), pp. 76–92.

[32] Here we can only refer in general to the fact that theology is more and more alive to the limitations imposed upon a truth by reason of the fact that the language in which it is formulated is conditioned by the period in history to which it belongs. Theology is in process of being freed from theories of language which do not necessarily have anything to do with the essential matter of the Church's faith. Behind the theory of the 'perfection' of ecclesiastical formulations lies a concept of the history of Christianity which has nowadays become untenable. For if it was forgotten that sacred history

infallibility of the Pope and that of the Church, this was more than an *ad hoc* solution.[33] The relevant declaration is couched in the language of the period: "The Roman Pontiff, when he speaks *ex cathedra* — that is, when, in the exercise of his office as pastor and teacher of all Christians he defines, by virtue of his supreme apostolic authority, a doctrine of faith or morals to be held by the whole Church — is, by reason of the divine assistance promised to him in Blessed Peter, possessed of that infallibility with which the divine Redeemer wished his Church to be endowed in defining doctrines of faith and morals; consequently such definitions of the Roman Pontiff are irreformable of their own nature *(ex sese),* and not by reason of the Church's consent."[34] In this definition too, then, the accent is clearly laid upon the promise, and so on the faithfulness of God.

From sacred Scripture, then, it is wholly evident that the question of the Church's infallibility is to be regarded from the stand-

develops towards an ultimate goal, in which its own perfection will be achieved, and if it was thought of as already in that stage of ultimate perfection, then this could not fail to influence men's ideas about the language in which it was expressed. A point which has a fundamental bearing on all this should be borne in mind here, that namely which A. Mirgeler draws attention to in his "Erfahrung in der Geschichte und Geschichtswissenschaft", in W. Strolz, ed., *Experiment und Erfahrung in Wissenschaft und Kunst* (1963), pp. 233 f., 249 f. It is that the Western idea of history is "encumbered from the outset" with an eschatological conception of history, and, by reason of the predominantly Roman tradition, "has a bias against the historical", *ibid.,* p. 249. The didactic pronouncement should also be viewed in the light of this conception of history.

[33] H. Küng, *Strukturen der Kirche,* p. 318, insists that there is in Catholic teaching an essential connection between the infallibility of the Church and the infallibility of the Church's official representatives (the Pope and the councils). That since in his Spirit Christ has promised that by the grace he has won by his eschatological victory he will guard the Church as a whole from falling away, he will also safeguard the official representatives of the Church as a group in their official capacity from falling away from faith, that is from any error in essential doctrine such as would radically distort the message of Christ. [34] *DS* 3074.

point of the unchangeable faithfulness of God, and that for man's part faithfulness to God in word and deed is demanded in view of this. And the perversity of those opinions which would tear 'doctrine' and 'life' apart from one another must also be apparent.

According to the witness of Scripture and tradition a bad shepherd is a curse, and a good one is a blessing. One must guard against the delusion that it is possible to fix upon a perfect formula which will determine finally and conclusively the question of Papal 'infallibility'. From the standpoint of Scripture the primacy will continue to represent a problem for the Church both in the abstract and in the concrete, either a blessing or a curse, either a danger or a support, according to whether or not the individual holders of the office prove to be 'faithful'.[35]

While, therefore, the evidence of the Bible itself demands that emphasis must be placed without qualification on the importance of faithfulness in the holder of the office, it must be no less firmly maintained on the basis of the same scriptural evidence that those who attempt to find a Donatist interpretation of the faithfulness required in the holder of office will search the inspired books for it in vain. Human infidelity has no power to impugn the 'indefectibility' in her official structure which has been promised to the Church by God, and which is based on the gift of the Holy Spirit. Both an exclusively Donatist interpretation of faithfulness in the holders of official positions, and a one-sided emphasis on the 'intellectual' infallibility attached to the official position itself (that is, in effect, a denial of the element of faithfulness to

---

[35] B. Brinkmann, *PhTh* 1 (1966), p. 117 raises the following objection to these observations: "But the infallibility of the pope does not depend upon the moral integrity of the bearer of the office at any given time." Apart from the fact that at no point in this book has it been maintained that papal infallibility does depend on the moral integrity of the bearer of the office at any given time, what is in question here is the fact that the Pope in the discharge of his office can no more be dispensed from his duty of faithfulness to the gospels than any other Christian, and the personal life of a Pope has a great influence.

the law of Christ in the practice of daily life) are to be regarded as inadmissible interpretations.

In this question of how infallibility should be conceived of Vatican II also stands in the line of tradition which we have been following here: Infallibility (truth, faithfulness, reliability) is promised to the Church as a whole, and none of the various aspects of infallibility — whether the infallibility of the Pope or that of the college of bishops — can be understood otherwise than as arising from the promise of God and the support of the Spirit of truth.[36]

A further point, apart from those which have already been mentioned, is that the question of the truth of Scripture is of profound significance for the religious life of each single individual. God's 'faithfulness' is extended to every member of his people. Every member finds the basis for his own individual relationship with God in the faithfulness promised on God's part. Through God's promise alone is the justification of the sinner achieved, and it is this faithfulness of God that provides the basis for the new faithfulness which man on his side exercises towards God (cf. Rom 3:1 ff.).

A deeper insight into the question of truth in the Bible has a further contribution to make, in that it can lead to a more accurate definition of the relationship between the Old and New Testaments, and one that conforms more closely to the findings of recent exegesis. Today the question is: How can we still maintain that the Old Testament has a valid relevance to the New, if we accept that in interpreting the Old Testament New Testament writers have followed methods which are appropriate only to one particular epoch, and which can no longer carry any conviction for us? Is there a 'sens chrétien de l'Ancien Testament'[37] at all

---

[36] Cf. K. Rahner's commentary on *Lumen Gentium,* art. 25, in H. Vorgrimler, ed., *Commentary on the Documents of Vatican II,* vol. I (1967), pp. 145 ff.

[37] Cf. P. Grelot, *Sens chrétien de l'Ancien Testament* (1962). Without bringing any new aspects of the problem to light C. Larcher, *L'Actualité chrétienne de l'Ancien Testament d'après le Nouveau Testament* (1962), continues with the old

in the former sense of the phrase? In other words we find our-selves confronted with the question of whether we are still committed to maintaining the New Testament view of the Old Testament even though we have come to recognize that the method of interpreting the Old Testament followed in the New has become unconvincing to us by reason of its being confined to one particular epoch.

Here too a return to the biblical concept of truth can contribute some enlightenment. For what the New Testament interpretation of the Old is based upon is the belief that in Jesus Christ God has proved himself faithful to his people, and has fulfilled his promises. How this is conveyed in detail in the New Testament by means of citations of Old Testament passages does admittedly depend on the methods of scriptural interpretation accepted at that time. But for this very reason what we should be concerned with is to recapture the spirit of this New Testament view of the Old Testament, and it would amount to a radical misconception if we set out to establish these New Testament methods of inter-preting the Old as absolutely and permanently valid in the sense that actually as methods they have binding force upon all Christians forever.

What is indeed binding for us is the faith of the Christians of the New Testament period, by which they saw the Old Testament as an historical preparation for the New Testament. These New Testament Christians thought of themselves as those to whom the God of the Old Testament had finally and conclusively revealed himself in Jesus Christ as the faithful and true God.[38]

approach to the problem in his discussion of this question. Cf. also F.-M. Braun, *Jean le Théologien. Les grandes traditions d'Israël et l'accord des écritures selon le quatrième évangile* (1964).
[38] C. Westermann, "Vergegenwärtigung der Geschichte in den Psalmen", *Zwischenstation — Festschrift K. Kupisch* (1963), pp. 263f.; W. Zimmerli, "Der Wahrheitserweis Jahwes nach der Botschaft der beiden Exilspropheten", pp. 150f.; further H. W. Wolff in C. Westermann, ed., *Zur Hermeneutik des AT: Theologische Bücherei, Nachdrucke und Berichte aus dem 20. Jahrhundert,* vol. XI (1963), pp. 140–80.

What is the underlying purpose of the New Testament interpretation of the Old Testament, in which the methods of interpretation generally accepted at the time were employed? It is to acknowledge the existence of a power which is all-pervasive in the history of Israel. This factor, which exercises a decisive influence upon each individual event is the faithfulness of God to his people.[39] For since the making of the covenant a continual 'event' has been taking place between the people and God, one which underlies all the individual events. This abiding relationship between the people and their covenant Lord continues in force only because God, for his part, having once made the pact, upholds it. Thus despite all infidelity on the part of the people in their history, the love of God for Israel continues changelessly to endure. God's faithfulness is his truth. In concluding his observations on the manifestation of Yahweh's truth in the prophets Ezekiel and Deutero-Isaiah W. Zimmerli uses words which magnificently convey the special character of the biblical concept of truth and its inseparable connection with the faithfulness of God: "The answers given by both prophets at the beginning and end of the period in which Israel reached her nadir are impressively uniform in tone: the word of Yahweh is the 'truth' that stands (yaqûm) when all else falls. But the word is not a word of which the meaning can be found in the realm of ideas. It is no demonstrable or theoretic truth of special profundity that it conveys. Rather it is the word that is wholly united to the event, the word that Yahweh himself interprets: 'I have spoken and I will do it.' It is the word which Yahweh stands by and so remains true to what he has promised. In this sense it is the word that proclaims that God is faithful. Ezekiel's mouth is opened at that point at which God, by his annihilating judgment, shows

---

[39] T. Vriezen, *Die Erwählung Israels nach dem Alten Testament* (1953), pp. 100 ff., 108: ". . . In the last analysis Yahweh has become known to her (Israel) only as the God of holy and faithful love"; see also H. Wildberger, *Jahwes Eigentumsvolk* (1960), pp. 110–13.

that he upholds the oracles of judgment proclaimed by his proph-ets. Deutero-Isaiah's exultation is aroused at that point at which God stands by what he has promised for his down-trodden people in a manner even more powerful than in those 'former things' of the exodus from Egypt (43:16ff.) and the point at which he makes himself known to his chosen people afresh. The prophet's message opens with a recognition which is to constitute a theme throughout it, namely that in contrast to the transience of all human glory, the 'truth' is that 'the word of our God *stands (yaqîm)* for ever' (40:6–8). And the closing words of the collection of sayings of Deutero-Isaiah return in a different form, and by means of a vivid image, to the same praise of the word of God, which endures in what it promises and accomplishes its work (55, 10f.) In the hour of her deepest deprivation Israel lives by this word alone. Yet this word, so puny as it seems, is the riches in comparison with which the splendour and 'triumph' of the world of idols all round can be made to look insignificant, so that 'strangers' acknowledge, dumbfounded, 'God is with you'."[40] Zimmerli goes on to observe that it is tempting to transfer our gaze from this prophet to what took place in the apostolic preaching. "Here rejoicing rises up once more over a situation in which, humanly speaking, the depths to which the people have sunk before the intervention of the Son is incompar-ably more desperate; and now rejoicing is accompanied by the knowledge that it ultimately holds good; that God does indeed stand by what he has said, and what he formerly spoke in promise that he will also perform."[41]

A characteristic of the covenant history is that in its details it cannot be deduced to be history in the true sense at all. But what becomes plainer to Israel in the course of time is her knowledge of God's faithfulness to his people, a fact which is proved pre-

---

[40] W. Zimmerli, "Der Wahrheitserweis Jahwes nach der Botschaft der beiden Exilspropheten", pp. 150f.
[41] *Ibid.*, p. 151.

cisely in situations which, humanly speaking, would be regarded as the end of the covenant.[42]

Thus the history of Israel affords us the unique spectacle of a development which takes two opposite courses. Whereas the tendency of the people's lives is away from the covenant, the faithfulness of God leads them back to the covenant again and again. Whereas the people break the covenant, God holds firm to it in that in ever increasing measure he submits to the test that faithfulness which he promised to show to Israel in the beginning, in new and unforeseen situations, even though he is in no way committed to do so by the terms of the covenant. The result is that in the history of the people of Israel what is presumed to be the end is in reality a fresh beginning. God's faithfulness stands clearly revealed in the course of time as the cause of her past, her present and her future.

With the making of the covenant, therefore, an historical movement is initiated the goal of which continues throughout the whole of time to lie in a future that is promised but still unfulfilled.[43] This radical openness of the covenant to a future all of which lies in the hands of the faithful God of Israel enables the first Christians to recognize in Jesus Christ the definitive fulfilment of the promises. In Jesus Christ they saw brought to its fulfilment that history which God had inaugurated when he made the covenant with his people. And again this same history of God with his people, together with its fulfilment in Christ, provided grounds for a new hope in the faithfulness promised by God when he said that he would remain with his own until the end of the ages.

It follows from what has been said that the relationship between the Old and New Testament is that of an *historical* connection

---

[42] Cf. C. Westermann in *Zwischenstation — Festschrift K. Kupisch* (1963), p. 257.
[43] On the discussion of promise in the Old Testament see H. Gross, "Zum Problem Verheißung und Erfüllung", *BZ* 3 (1959), pp. 3–17; H. W. Wolff, *Das Geschichtsverständnis der alttestamentlichen Prophetie, Theologische Bücherei*, vol. XI (1963), pp. 319–40.

in that the people are the same, and the covenant which determines its history is the same.

This close historical involvement between the Old and New Testaments provides the conditions for a profound influence of the language of the Old Testament upon that of the New,[44] for since the language and literature of a people, once formed, play a decisive part in determining the course of its history, it follows that the language finds fresh expression in that history itself. In this respect there is an intimate and irremovable interconnection between language and history.

If we take with due seriousness the connection which we have found between the two Testaments, then we shall have our eyes open to the further fact that an historical development entails changes which come about unexpectedly, and which may have very far-reaching effects. Thus with regard to the relationship between the Old and New Testament we should view the developments which have occurred in the course of history without any attempts at false harmonization.

In practice, therefore, any explanation of the connection between the Old and New Testament which relies upon the sort of allegorizing appropriate only to one particular epoch will thereby fail,[45] for such an explanation must advert not only to those factors which unite the two Testaments, but also to the cleavages and contradictions between them. More justice can be done to the factor of periodic renewal by treating of the history of Israel than by the allegorizing interpretation of Scripture. The element in the history of the people of Israel that astonishes us is not so much the contradictions, the inconsistencies or obscurities of expression in the word which have been handed

---

[44] Cf. G. von Rad, *Theologie des Alten Testaments,* vol. II (3rd ed., 1962), pp. 364 ff.

[45] R. Gögler, *Zur Theologie des biblischen Wortes bei Origenes* (1963), p. 392, remarks, e. g., on the allegorizing of Origen: "The allegorizing of Origen is far from being the most important and most noteworthy feature of his method of treating the word of the Bible. We cannot return to this."

down to us; rather it is the still deeper unity of the 'true-ness' (faithfulness) of God, which shines through the imperfections.

In accordance with what has been said we can only invoke as the chief rule for correctly viewing the connection between the Old and New Testaments that laid down by the apostle Paul: the Old Testament is to be understood in the light of the New Testament gift of the Spirit (cf. 2 Cor 3:12ff.), i.e. he who wishes to grasp the real relationship between the two Testaments must first apprehend the Spirit that causes the movement in history of which we have been speaking.[46] At the same time it must be borne in mind that any given account of the connection between the two Testaments is subject to the limitations of its own epoch, and may not therefore be taken in an absolute and permanent sense.

The covenant made by God with his people, and the faithfulness on God's part of which the people were assured also have a decisive influence upon the language of the Bible.[47] The most immediately striking characteristic of biblical language is its anthropomorphisms. But so far as human understanding is concerned these constitute a stone of stumbling. Philosophy strives to replace these anthropomorphisms, which it considers

---

[46] U. Horst, "Exegese und Fundamentaltheologie", *MTZ* 16 (1965), pp. 198f., rightly points out that the most radical reason for the tension which exists between theology and exegesis lies in the fact that revelation is conceived of as a mechanical process; according to this conception what is initially revealed is sentences, dogmas and rules, that is truths from which further truths can be deduced by logic, and not the event and the mystery of Jesus Christ.

[47] In this respect the explanations of W. Zimmerli in his article, "Die Weisung des Alten Testaments zum Geschäft der Sprachen", *Gottes Offenbarung — Gesammelte Aufsätze* (1963), pp. 277–99, are not very fruitful. The observations of K. Löwith, "Die Sprache als Vermittler von Mensch und Welt", *Gesammelte Abhandlungen. Zur Kritik der geschichtlichen Existenz* (1960), pp. 208–27, are more penetrating. H. Gollwitzer, *Die Existenz Gottes im Bekenntnis des Glaubens* (6th ed., 1963), pp. 113f., offers certain basic considerations on the language of the Bible and its anthropomorphisms. On biblical anthropomorphism see also E. L. Cherbonnier in *HTR* 55 (1962), pp. 187–206.

as mere primitive figures of speech concerning God, with pure abstract ideas.[48] But in this philosophy takes up a position which, linguistically speaking, is in opposition to the Bible. When philosophy wants to rid the Bible of its anthropomorphic expressions for God, or attempts to find substitutes for them, it is, in effect, refusing to recognize the limits imposed on human understanding by the anthropomorphisms of the Bible. What they convey is indeed a message of God to man, but they describe and transmit this utterance of God only in human and anthropomorphic terms. The question of whether, in view of this, God really did speak to Israel at Sinai in the manner described in the biblical narrative can therefore be answered: another account also anthropomorphic in character is indeed conceivable, and the possibility does exist that another tradition concerning the event was also current in Israel. But it is impossible to arrive at an account that is free from anthropomorphisms; and if this is true, then a scientifically exact account of the words which God spoke to Moses is thereby excluded.[49]

[48] From the 17th century onwards the anthropomorphisms of the Old Testament have been a particularly irritating thorn in the side of the 'enlightened', which they want to get rid of: see M. Geiger, *Geschichtsmächte oder Evangelium?* (1953), pp. 84ff.; H. Gollwitzer, *Die Existenz Gottes im Bekenntnis des Glaubens,* pp. 123 ff.

[49] Gollwitzer, *ibid.,* p. 117, formulates the problem in his own terms as follows: "When the Lord of Israel bestows himself by his revelation he does indeed do so according to the linguistic conditions appropriate to the particular mode of existence of the recipients of his revelation, but not according to the conditions of their mode of cognition: This is precisely the distinction that must be observed. If he had bestowed himself according to these latter conditions, then he would be as wholly ascertainable as an object in a room, subject to our judgment and apprehension; in him existence and essence would be distinct, i.e. he would have a 'thing-like' mode of existence, which we could ascertain without thereby being brought into his presence, subjected to his judgment and grace, to decide whether we were for or against him. He would not be the Lord who bestows knowledge of himself as the free gift of his grace, and who has no existence which makes him 'be-for-us' as the object of our knowledge apart from that 'being-for-us' which is the gift of his grace."

It is the *covenant* that makes it possible to speak of God in anthropomorphisms. By it God entered into a particular kind of union. Henceforward he is the Lord — Israel his servant; he is the Father — they are his children; he is the judge who condemns and acquits — they are the accused. Since the making of the covenant, therefore, it is possible to speak of God in human terms and, to be specific, "indirectly, i.e. this speech takes the form not of a description of his nature, but of witness to his deeds and the proclamation and exaltation of his will. And yet there can be direct speech too in that men can speak directly to him and directly with him in virtue of the fact that his coming has made it possible for them to enter into communion with him. Words can be spoken to him but also of him, about him; admittedly they can be so spoken only by those whom he has in view, who stand before him, are in his presence. Statements cannot be made about him, therefore, as an objective being existing 'in himself'. The ultimate reason why statements of this sort cannot be made about him is that in relation to an object which has an existence 'of itself' of this sort I too exist 'of myself', i.e. unseen by and isolated from it. Now it is not true that I exist unseen by and isolated from God."[50]

In the Bible taken as a whole, preference is given to particular and concrete modes of speech rather than to universal and abstract ones, and personal modes are preferred to impersonal and objective ones. "Preference" implies "that the mode of speech which is not preferred is not thereby absolutely excluded, but must be taken only in relation to the other mode which has priority over it, and upon which it must depend for its full significance."[51] The statements about God in the Bible are based upon God's condescension to man, on the historical events in which God encounters his people in the concrete, until at last a new communion with God is attained to, and a new covenant

[50] *Ibid.*, p. 118.
[51] *Ibid.*, p. 122.

with men is instituted through his Son, Jesus Christ. The choice of language is determined by the nature of the events to which it refers; hence the concreteness and humanity of this history of God with his people is projected into the language too. The manner in which God bestows himself is that which is normal in encounters between men. Hence in Scripture man's union with him is characterized as one of hearing, obeying, believing, praising, loving and thanking etc. Thus the language of Israel is moulded by its history and, since the two influence each other mutually, the language itself in its turn has an influence upon the history. In this way the continuity of that history is preserved. For when the Israelites seek the protection of God, they recount his deeds of the past, and this is an expression of their faith in the faithfulness of God which still endures, and which shows itself to be 'true' in this new situation of need.[52] Thus the preference for anthropomorphisms in Scripture and, together with this the emphasis on the 'truth' (in the sense of 'faithfulness') of God is conditioned by the mutual influence of history and language upon each other, which is such a predominant feature. God is the faithful Lord and Father of his people. His faithfulness is the subject of Israel's hymns of praise.

Since the covenant between God and the people has provided a basis for a new union between them, and therefore too a language cast in a particular mould, this is necessarily projected into the literature of Israel and affects this also. The literary traditions as they were handed down were kept free from all that was contrary to the spirit of the covenant. The spirit that excludes all belief in strange gods — that same spirit lives on in all branches of Israel's literary tradition. Israel knows of myths, but these are purged of their polytheistic elements. Yahweh takes the place of the assembly of the gods. In this way the myth was blended into the history of the chosen people as a subordinate element,

---

[52] Cf. C. Westermann, "Vergegenwärtigung der Geschichte in den Psalmen", p. 257.

and any feature which might have had a bad effect on Israel's indigenous tradition was purged from it.[53] By taking over the myths in this way, guided always by the spirit of faith in Yahweh, Israel was enabled to hand down valuable knowledge.[54] This same faith in the unique God of the covenant extends its dominant influence to the promulgation of the laws, the history writing, prophecy and wisdom literature,[55] the psalms and the 'love song' of Hebrew literature, which acknowledges no heathen goddess of love. In the case of the New Testament writings the situation is similar. Throughout all their range and variation they bear witness to the faith of their composers in Jesus Christ. They are intended to record what Jesus did and taught (cf. Acts 1:1). For testimony of this kind even a simple communication such as the Epistle to Philemon has a contribution to make. A place is given to it in the canon because in its own modest way it bears witness to the spirit of the whole no less than a major theological treatise such as, for instance, the Epistle to the Romans. Despite the profound differences between the various sections of the New Testament, here too the language in all of them remains the same.

The biblical concept of 'truth' also opens the way to a deeper insight into the relationship which exists between the person

[53] The myth threatens, encloses man with his life in history within a cycle of eternal return to the same point. See. W. Emrich, *Protest und Verheißung* (2nd ed., 1963), p. 262. This danger is avoided by the fact that the myth is inserted into a preconceived course of history such as that which the history of the people of Israel represents. On the question of myth and revelation cf., among others, A. Anwander, *Zum Problem des Mythos* (1954).

[54] A. Mirgeler, "Erfahrung in der Geschichte", pp. 250 f., points out that throughout the first eleven chapters of Genesis the memory of an earlier heathen history is apparent, and thereby also, to a very limited extent, an awareness of a universal history of the past, one that embraces mankind as a whole.

[55] W. Zimmerli, "Ort und Grenze der Weisheit im Rahmen der alttestamentlichen Theologie", *Gottes Offenbarung. Gesammelte Aufsätze zum A.T.* (1963), pp. 306 ff.

166

of Jesus Christ and the canonical Scriptures. In Jesus Christ the manifold forms in which God speaks and acts towards Israel have come to their fulfilment. "In many and various ways God spoke of old to our fathers by the prophets; but in these last days he has spoken to us by a Son" (Heb 1:1). According to Semitic thought, therefore, what is asserted of the truth of God is now transferred to Jesus Christ. The 'truth' of God's words to Israel hitherto now finds its consummation in the word of the Father through the Son, and the confirmation of the words of the Son through the works of the Father. Christ himself, therefore, is called the 'truth'.[56] Jesus is the 'truth' in that by his death and resurrection he has manifested the 'true-ness' (faithfulness) of God to Israel. A further outcome of this is that the preaching of the words and works of Jesus is also called the 'gospel of truth'.[57] Expressed in biblical language all this can be formulated as follows: the truth, the inerrancy of Scripture *is* Jesus Christ. For through him God has been revealed as he who is faithful. In this connection, however, it must be borne in mind that in Jesus Christ a new promise has been given by God. He will come again. The words which God speaks to men are fulfilled indeed, but not finally done with, as though the matter they referred to had been conclusively finished. For its ultimate consummation the 'truth' of God still awaits the return of the Son. Until then the 'truth' of Scripture remains essentially the subject of faith. Faith in its turn is determined by the 'truth' of God.[58] It is man's response to God's 'true-ness' through Christ and in Christ. It is the 'yes' evoked by a recognition of that truth which, due regard being had to the exigencies of language,

---

[56] Jn 14:6; Eph 4:21.
[57] Cf. I. de la Potterie, "Jésus et la vérité d'après Eph. 4:21", *Studiorum Paulinorum Congressus Internationalis Catholicus 1961,* vol. II (1963), p. 45, n. 7, pp. 54 ff.
[58] Cf. N. Weiser, R. Bultmann: *TWNT,* vol. VI, pp. 174–230; I. Alfaro, "Fides in terminologia biblica", *Gregorianum* 42 (1961), pp. 462-505; C. Butler, "The Object of Faith according to St. Paul's Epistles", *Studiorum Paulinorum Congressus Internationalis Catholicus 1961,* vol. I (1963), pp. 15–30.

is meant to be binding in faith for members of a human community and to this end is expressed in written form.[59] Finally it is the belief that God's 'true-ness' will be ultimately and fully revealed in the return of Jesus Christ.

[59] Butler, *ibid.*, p. 29.

CONCLUSION

The inerrancy of Scripture is a postulate of Christian theology which, having for a long period been accepted as true without dispute, has, with the emergence of the modern age, been radically called in question, rejected and denied. The result of this state of affairs for theology and exegesis is that it is necessary to enquire into what really is the tradition of the Church which is binding for the faithful. An investigation of the whole complex problem leads to the recognition that the general conception upheld in theological schools concerning the inerrancy of the Bible contains elements which have found their way into Christian theology at that point at which for the first time it became open to pagan influences. The line can be traced back to Philo and Augustine. The decisive factor now is that the concept of truth upheld by this theology that goes back to Philo and Augustine superimposes on Scripture a perfectionist ideal of truth which is foreign to the Bible itself. According to this concept of truth the Bible is a holy book containing perfect knowledge, and its statements concerning history and nature are in accordance with a truth which is unimpeachable.

The truth claimed by the canonical writings of the Old and New Testament is of a quite different nature. He who realizes that the attempt made here to accept the Hebrew language on its own terms in this question of truth is more than a mere philological game — he is prepared to see in language the wonderful means by which nature, world and God are disclosed to man. We are far from creating a false mystique about the Hebrew language or what is alleged to be Hebrew thought. On the contrary, the situation is this: the concept of truth current among the Israelites is a Semitic one. The Hebrews held, in common with the other Semites of the ancient Near East, a concept of truth which places the emphasis on reliability, faithfulness. But through the covenant of God with Israel this concept of truth acquires new dimensions, dimensions which derive from the history of God with his people. God manifests his 'true-ness' (faithfulness) by standing by his people, and fulfilling his word. Christ is the mediator of a new and final covenant, and, as the fulfilment of all the words of God, he is 'truth itself'.[1] It follows that the scriptural concept of truth is different from that which is often maintained in Western theology, for the claim that it puts forward is that it speaks of an unchanging fidelity of God to his people and to his words.

Regarded from this point of view, the emergence of a new epoch of history in Europe which has called in question that which tradition presupposes, has necessitated a radical re-appraisal of the concept of scriptural inerrancy maintained hitherto. A factor which has caused confusion in this controversy up to the present is that justified criticisms of untenable theories of inspiration and inerrancy have often been combined with a complete refusal to recognize any revelation at all. The only effect of this has been that the defenders of the traditional theories have found confirmation in their views.

The question of the truth of Scripture must now be seen in its radical involvement in the history of Israel and the Church. The truth of Scripture represents one particular aspect of the

---

[1] I. de la Potterie in *NRT* 88 (1966), p. 165: ". . . he is the truth not in the sense employed by the Greeks, who intended to signify thereby that he is God; but in the biblical sense: in him, the man Jesus, who is at the same time the Son of God, the plenitude of revelation is made present to us."

170

indefectibility of the Church. The indefectibility of the Church is bound up with its very existence as the people of God. In this connection the problem of the intellectual aspect of enduring truth, steadfastness, deserves special notice. What has to be seen here is that it is just as harmful to exaggerate this aspect of indefectibility as to under-estimate it. This lies in the nature of the case. A deeper insight into the real extent of the biblical concept of 'true-ness', 'faithfulness' has the further effect of affording us a view of the Old and New Testament as a single whole, which is more in conformity with our mode of thought. At the same time it opens the way to that belief which is always alive in the Church, that Christ is the centre of Scripture.

The decisions of Vatican II regarding the truth of sacred Scripture will have significant and far-reaching consequences. They set the Church on a course which will lead to overcoming misunderstandings which have lasted since the trial of Galileo.

INDEX OF AUTHORS

See also Bibliography

173

174

SUBJECT INDEX

Prepared by David J. Bourke

178